THE FORMATION OF
THE NEW TESTAMENT

THE UNIVERSITY OF CHICAGO PRESS
CHICAGO, ILLINOIS

———

THE BAKER & TAYLOR COMPANY
NEW YORK

THE MACMILLAN COMPANY OF CANADA, LIMITED
TORONTO

THE CAMBRIDGE UNIVERSITY PRESS
LONDON

THE MARUZEN-KABUSHIKI-KAISHA
TOKYO, OSAKA, KYOTO, FUKUOKA, SENDAI

THE MISSION BOOK COMPANY
SHANGHAI

THE FORMATION OF THE NEW TESTAMENT

By

EDGAR J. GOODSPEED

Professor of Biblical and Patristic Greek
The University of Chicago

THE UNIVERSITY OF CHICAGO PRESS
CHICAGO

1926

Composed and Printed By
The University of Chicago Press
Chicago, Illinois, U.S.A.

TO DONALD P. BEAN
COUNSELOR AND FRIEND

PREFACE

AMONG the problems of the New Testament one of the greatest is the New Testament itself. How did twenty-seven scattered letters and pamphlets come to find one another and be gathered into the New Testament? How did they come to survive until this process guaranteed their lasting preservation?

How did this Christian collection so soon achieve equality with and even superiority to the earlier Jewish Bible? How did it come to be called the New Covenant or Testament, leaving the inferior title Old Testament to the Jewish scriptures? How did it come to include four different gospels, all regarded as of equal authority?

In *The Story of the New Testament*, I have tried to tell how the several books of the New Testament came to be written. But when all these books were written there was still no New Testament. How did it come to be?

As a collection the New Testament is a social product. It grew out of the needs and moods of the early churches. It is not so much a collection of individual books as a collection of collections. Groups of letters or gospels were formed here and there; these groups were afterwards gathered into a larger group, and this in turn again enlarged, in the face of steadfast conservative opposition, into our New Testament. These group stages in the formation of the New Testament help in the understanding of the process.

Certain places, too, made particular contributions to the process. At Ephesus the earliest considerable groups were formed, though at a time long before a New Testament was thought of. At Rome these groups were first combined, and at Alexandria, against the wishes of Rome and Antioch, the collection thus formed was enlarged. Church councils had very little to do with it; practical needs and great personalities had much more.

We are witnessing a great increase in intelligent interest in the New Testament, its origin, and its message. Many thoughtful people are keenly interested in how the New Testament arose; who selected the books, and on what grounds some were chosen and others left out. In response to this interest, and in the hope of analyzing a little more definitely the process of the formation of the New Testament, this book is written. EDGAR J. GOODSPEED

July 5, 1926

CONTENTS

I

THE OLD TESTAMENT AND
THE NEW

THE books of the New Testament were written by various hands, at various places in the Greek world, and at various times between 50 and 150 A.D.[1] They meet us, most of them, toward the year 200 assembled into a collection —the New Testament.[2] How did this come about? What caused these particular books of all others to be selected? How did they find one another and take on the authority of Holy Scripture? What steps can be traced in this extraordinary historical development, which gave to the world the Christian Bible?

Christianity began as a religion of the spirit. The primitive believers sought guidance from within, believing that in their own hearts the Spirit of God had taken up its abode, and that it would guide them to the truth.[3] In accepting the authority of a collection of books they sacrificed this early attitude, and seemed to go to the opposite extreme. What occasioned this remarkable change, which concerned something so central in early Christian religious thought?

These questions are rising in the minds of many thoughtful people. To answer them it is necessary to recall the life and problems of the first centuries of the Christian Era, and to examine the Christian writings of those early centuries for the light they may throw upon them.

The idea of inspired books expressing the will of God was a common one in antiquity. The Romans religiously preserved the Sibylline books, which were believed to be the inspired utterances of the ancient prophetess, the Sibyl, and were consulted by special religious officers in times of crisis. They were of Greek origin and were written in Greek verse, and while they were never officially published (being considered too sacred for that), for a long time before and after Christ they exerted a great deal of influence upon religion at Rome. In Egypt, in early Christian times, the forty-two sacred Books of Hermes described the religious duties and observances of the ancient Egyptian religion.[4] Other religions of the time had their sacred books.[5]

But it was the Jewish Bible that constituted the background of the formation of the Christian New Testament. The Old Testament was the mother of the New. In the Jewish circles in

2

which Christianity arose, belief in a written revelation of the will of God was deeply rooted. The divine inspiration of their scriptures was, in fact, the most characteristic doctrine of Jewish thought in the time of Jesus. Christianity grew up in the presence of this doctrine, and was profoundly influenced by it.

Of course the Jews did not think of their Bible as the Old Testament. They called it the Writings, or Scriptures. Josephus, who wrote his Antiquities about 93 A.D., tells us that the Jews of Palestine accepted twenty-two books of scripture.[6] But they counted Ruth as part of Judges; Nehemiah as part of Ezra; Lamentations as part of Jeremiah; Samuel, Kings, and Chronicles as one book each, and the twelve minor prophets as one book, so that their twenty-two books included all that later Judaism counted as twenty-four and that we count as thirty-nine. Their purpose in doing this was apparently to hold the number to that of the letters in the Hebrew alphabet, and thus indicate its complete and unalterable character. These books were scripture, and no others could be added to the list. Another way of counting made Ruth, the Song of Songs, Ecclesiastes, Lamentations, and Esther one book, and still arrived at the same total, which was evidently of great importance in Jewish eyes. We shall see the influence of this number in more than one early form of the New Testament.

Josephus, like the Pharisees of his day, divided these books into three groups: the five books of Moses, thirteen books of the prophets, and four books of hymns and precepts—meaning probably Psalms, Job, Proverbs, and Ecclesiastes.

These were all divinely inspired scriptures, but they were not all on the same level in Jewish esteem. The Law of Moses—the first five books of the Old Testament—stood highest. It was from heaven, given directly by God. Moses did not write one verse of his own knowledge. The prophetic books were regarded with a reverence not quite so extreme, and the hymns and precepts were in turn inferior to them in sanctity.

In these differences may be traced the growth of the Hebrew scriptures. In the times of Ezra and Nehemiah, 444 B.C., the Mosaic Law was the Jewish Bible. In the two centuries that followed, the histories and sermons of the prophets were gathered into a second collection of almost equal sanctity. In Jesus' time the third group of writings, the hymns and precepts, was

4

just being admitted to the Jewish Bible, very much as the Prayer-Book and the Hymnbook are often found bound up with old printings of the English Bible; but these were probably not definitely recognized as part of the Jewish scriptures until the synod of Jamnia, about 90 A.D. By the time Josephus wrote his books at Rome, the contents of the Jewish Bible of Palestine were definitely settled. The three groups were generally recognized, and the Pharisees at least held to the pre-eminence of the Mosaic Law, and ascribed to it the authority of verbal inspiration.

But the Jews were not confined in New Testament times to Palestine. There were great numbers of them out in the Greek world, in Egypt, Syria, Asia Minor, Greece, and the west, and the attitude of these Greek-speaking Jews toward their Bible had much to do with the formation of the New Testament. Their most influential center was at Alexandria, and there they had produced for missionary and other religious purposes a Greek translation of their Hebrew scriptures, which was known as the Septuagint.[7] Out in the Greek west, which was inclined to respect the Sibylline books and Eastern wisdom generally, the Septuagint came to be well known and to have wide influence.

The Greek Jews included in their scriptures a much larger circle of books than did the Jews of Palestine. Interspersed among the Jewish books of our Old Testament, our oldest manuscripts of the Greek Bible contain the Wisdom of Solomon, the Wisdom of Sirach, Judith, Tobit, and the four books of Maccabees.

Not only did the Jews out in the Greek world differ from those of Palestine in the contents of their Bible; they differed among themselves as to just what books belonged to it. That is, the Septuagint list or canon was never definitely settled. The Greek scripture was at once much more extensive, and much less uniform in contents, than that which prevailed in Palestine.

The Greek scripture differed from that of Palestine not only in contents, but in the way in which it was regarded. The Pharisaic idea of the verbal inspiration of the Law of Moses was extended by the Greek Jews to their whole body of scripture. This committed them to the position that it was all capable of religious use, and this in turn led them to resort to allegory in interpreting its meaning. This method had already been applied to Homer by the Stoic interpreters of his poems, and was not unknown in Palestine. But in the effort to harmonize their scripture with the best thought of their time, and to gain from every part of it the maximum of religious edification, the Greek Jews, under the leadership of Philo, carried this method of interpretation so far that it exercised a marked influence on later Christian interpretation and still controls much of our modern thinking about the Old Testament.

Almost from the first the Christians adopted the Jewish Bible. Jesus himself showed an instinctive reverence for it. He often appealed to its great statements of moral principle, and in the crises of his life found guidance and support in its commands and promises. On the other hand, Jesus did not hesitate to condemn the divorce law of Deuteronomy, the law of retaliation, and the Levitical food regulations. His teaching as to the Sabbath, too, was a decided change not simply from that of the rabbis but from that of the Old Testament. While Jesus' relation to the prophetic spirit in the Old Testament is close, he was far from giving to the Old Testament as a whole the unqualified assent natural to a Jew of his day. His attitude is a discriminating one, combining eager acceptance of its statements of enduring spiritual truth and free criticism of its moral imperfections.

Paul's appeal to the Old Testament is more frequent and confident. He repudiates the Jewish Law just as sweepingly as Jesus did. At the same time he claims the support of scripture for many of his teachings. Paul insists on the believer's freedom from the Law, but he readily accepts much that stands in the Law. His objection to the Law was less to its moral content than to the Jewish claim that it was religiously all-sufficient. In short, Paul accepts the teachings of the Old Testament, except where they conflict with his own experience and convictions. On such matters he follows his own convictions, finding in them an authority superior to that of scripture.

The books of the New Testament show a decided development in the degree of regard which their several writers feel for the Old Testament. From the free critical treatment of it on the part of Jesus, and the very modified authority which Paul ascribes to it, the Old Testament returns in the hands of later New Testament writers to its larger Jewish claims. The principle is at length fully stated in II Timothy: "All scripture is divinely inspired, and useful in teaching, in reproof, in correcting faults, and in training in uprightness."[8] This was precisely the principle which forced upon those who held it, whether Jews or Christians, the allegorical interpretation of the Old Testament. For there were many stories and sayings in the Old Testament which suggested no moral lesson, until allegorically explained. So far from the position of Jesus had the Christian view of the Old Testament already gone; and so completely was the New Testament written under the shadow of the Old.

II

THE AIMS OF THE EARLIEST
CHRISTIAN WRITERS

WHAT did the writers of the earliest Christian books think of their writings? Were they conscious that they were writing scripture? What did they think of one another's writings? These questions call for the best answers we can find for them before we go on to ask what later generations thought of these books.

Early Christianity shows that reawakening of religious intuitions which is characteristic of every great religious movement. Jesus had boldly revised the ideals of religion, and his personality and teaching had profoundly impressed his followers. He had aroused in them a new religious life, and in its inward promptings they found the expression of his spirit. He pointed them to hidden springs of religious inspiration within themselves, and thus enfranchised their religious intuitions, and stimulated their inner life. This found varied expression: first, in their religious meetings; and later, when the Christian movement reached the Greek world, it began to overflow in writing.

Paul did not expect his letters to be preserved or collected, still less to be regarded as Holy Scripture. He wrote them with no literary intention but simply to meet immediate local needs in various pressing situations in his work of preaching the gospel among the Greeks. That new loyalty to the inner life which Jesus had demanded is seen at work in Paul. Upon some matters he spoke with what he felt to be the authority of the divine spirit. This was no mere manner of speaking with him, for he is sometimes very careful to absolve the spirit from responsibility for views which he himself held and recommended.[1]

Paul does not say much about the sayings of Jesus, but when he does mention them, he speaks as though obedience to them were a matter of course. This is also the attitude of the earliest gospel, the Gospel of Mark. Jesus there appears as a commanding figure, filled with the divine spirit which made his teaching authoritative. Mark has little to say about his own authority. No gospel reveals less of the figure behind it or claims less for him. Of course the evangelist regarded his book as a trustworthy record, but its authority is only such as it might claim as the vehicle of Jesus' teaching. The writer has withdrawn himself almost entirely from the picture.

Mark was the basis of the later gospels, and their writers did not hesitate to take up into their works almost everything that his gospel contained.[2] But neither Matthew nor Luke had any hesitation about rearranging the events related by Mark, and Matthew often combined other materials with those supplied by him. In short, Mark is used by these later evangelists with great freedom. For the substance of his gospel Matthew was dependent upon sources, most if not all of them written, and his respect for them, Mark among the rest, did not prevent him from using them in a very free way. Matthew did not simply copy Mark; he made constant efforts to improve Mark, in general and in detail. He rearranged Mark's material to suit his larger purpose, and condensed or expanded his accounts, combining with them material from other sources and retouching them in his own skilful way. He evidently valued Mark as a useful and indeed indispensable source for the life of Jesus, but nothing more. Matthew very frequently quotes from the Old Testament in which he expressly recognized the voice of God, speaking through the prophets. He used Mark much more than he did the Old Testament, but never mentioned the fact, nor appealed to Mark as an authoritative work like the writings of the prophets. Mark had not at that early time risen to the position of scripture.

For his own work, the writer of the Gospel of Matthew, while he wrote with confidence, made no claim beyond the obvious historical and religious one natural to such an undertaking. The evangelist Luke had a much more explicitly historical purpose. With the aid of earlier accounts, including Mark, and after personal investigation, he produced the two volumes known to us as the Gospel of Luke and the Acts of the Apostles. It was his express intention[3] to improve upon the work of his predecessors, and while he was much more faithful to Mark's order and forms of statement than Matthew was, he omitted more of Mark than Matthew did. He treated Mark very much as he did his other sources, and he certainly had no especial reverence for it.

It is in the Gospel of John that this untrammeled use of the earlier Christian writings is most clear. Its author was well acquainted with the Gospel of Mark and probably that of Luke, and made free use of them in writing his own. But his resemblances to them are greatly outweighed by his differences from them. In his great effort to restate Christian truth in Greek terms he departs widely from the positions of the earlier evangelists and he differs from them in many important historical particulars. The writings of his predecessors had no more sacredness or scriptural authority for John than Mark had for Matthew or Luke. He had no scruple about changing and correcting their material.[4] In fact, it was in part in order to do this that he wrote.

But before the Gospel of John was written, a book had appeared in the region of Ephesus making much greater claims. It was the Revelation of John. With its opening words it describes itself as a prophecy, and to this claim it returns in its closing lines. The book is recommended for public reading in the churches, a blessing is pronounced upon anyone who reads it publicly, and on those who hear it read,[5] and a curse is laid upon anyone who may alter the book.[6] The writer, John, is evidently a prophet, and if his prophetic vocation be acknowledged, it is a natural conclusion that his book is inspired prophecy and therefore scripture. The striking thing is that it is so intended, and by virtue of this fact claims for itself a place of permanent authority, side by side with the Jewish scriptures.

In this new type of Christian literature we see the welding of the new prophetic sense of inward spiritual endowment with the old Jewish idea of inspired books. It thus foreshadows a Christian scripture. Alone among the books of the New Testament the Revelation claims for its whole contents the authority of divine inspiration.

The Letter to the Ephesians speaks of being built on the foundation of the apostles and prophets, and of God's spirit as disclosing the secret of Christ to the apostles and prophets, and thus reflects the respect with which Christian apostles and prophets were already regarded in its time.[7] They were naturally thought of as the ones through whom Christ spoke: through the apostles historically, through the prophets by the inspiration of his spirit. The Revelation of John shows the same great esteem for prophets and apostles. In its visions the wall of the city has twelve foundations and on them are the names of the twelve apostles of the

Lamb. Prophets and apostles were becoming authorities for the early churches.

Of course there had been prophets in the Christian circles from the first. Paul has much to say of such endowments among the Corinthians, where it was quite the usual thing for a "revelation" to be uttered at a meeting of the church. Christian prophets are spoken of in Acts, a book written only a short time before the Revelation. So when in the closing days of Domitian's reign the prophet John put his message in written form and called it a "prophecy," the innovation, great as it was, was quite in line with the familiar idea that Jesus' words were of the highest authority, and that by the spirit of God he still spoke to the churches. This thought is very clearly expressed in the Revelation, for it is Jesus who appears to the prophet and dictates the letters to the churches and who at the close of the book gives it his indorsement. The prophecy thus claims the authority of Jesus in a much larger measure than the gospels had done. They were authoritative in so far as they reported what Jesus said. But the Revelation claims throughout the authority of Jesus or his spirit. It is evident that the written revelations of Christian prophets played an important part in accustoming the early churches to the idea of Christian scripture side by side with Jewish.

This great welling up of the inner religious life soon found expression in other revelations. A generation later, Hermas, a Roman Christian, committed his visions to writing and they long exerted a widespread influence.[8] About the same time another Christian writer put forth a revelation in the name of the apostle Peter.[9] This was widely accepted for a time and continued to have some influence in the Middle Ages, and, in the churches of Abyssinia, even to modern times. Both these books had a place for a time in the New Testament, and it will be interesting to see how they lost it.

In writing to the Corinthians, Paul speaks of the leading figures in the church as apostles, prophets, and teachers.[10] His own message is that of the apostle. The Revelation of John claims the authority of the prophet. The third type is represented by the Letter to the Hebrews. Its writer makes no apostolic or prophetic claim, but speaks with confidence as a teacher. He has a high idea of the worth of his message; it is not a thing for the undeveloped or immature. He refuses to go back and discuss with his readers the rudiments of Christianity.[11]

His task is to present advanced and highly developed teaching, like the Melchizedek priesthood of Christ. His letter is an exhortation such as the synagogue authorities at Antioch asked Paul and Barnabas to make before that congregation. It is as such an appeal that this Christian teacher regards his letter.

The Epistle of James is very evidently a Christian sermon which was published by being addressed to the "twelve tribes that are scattered over the world." The writer makes no claim of authority, apostolic or prophetic. The letters of John are confident in tone, but base their appeal on the writer's religious experience and personal relations with those to whom he writes.

The pastoral epistles and I and II Peter definitely claim apostolic authors, and very distinctly mean to be regarded as authoritative by those who read them. II Peter is evidently built up about Jude, which forms the nucleus of it.[12] This shows that the writer of II Peter had Jude, but that it possessed for him no more sanctity than Mark had for the writers of the gospels of Matthew and Luke. II Peter also refers explicitly to the letters of Paul which have not only been collected in its day but are even regarded as scripture.[13] Indeed, they have

18

become a matter of controversy, for some Christian faction has adopted them as its favorite authorities. II Peter also shows acquaintance with the four gospels and with I Peter.[14] No other New Testament writer possessed any such Christian library. For in it were the collected gospels, the collected letters of Paul, and certainly two of our Catholic epistles, Jude and I Peter. It needed only the Acts and the Revelation to make it equal to the primitive New Testament.

Thus the New Testament itself reveals something of the stages by which it arose to its position of authority. It was not the claims of these ancient books that brought about their collection into the New Testament; few of them claimed any such distinction for themselves. The words of the Lord Jesus were their earliest standard, and then the voice of his spirit in the hearts of his first followers, the apostles and prophets, came to be regarded as having the same authority. His teaching and their revelations within a century after the first Christian book was written were considered Christian authorities equal to those of the Old Testament. What were the steps that led to their development into a book of Christian scripture?

III

THE FIRST COLLECTIONS: THE LETTERS OF PAUL

THERE is nothing in the Acts of the Apostles to suggest that Paul ever wrote a letter. And yet the Acts is our chief source for the life and work of Paul, and was written after and probably long after his letters were written. But those letters which we prize so highly evidently made no impression upon the writer of Acts, for he betrays no acquaintance with any of them. In fact, it is rather difficult sometimes to harmonize his picture of Paul's views with what Paul's letters tell us.

This can mean only one thing. When Acts was written, the letters of Paul had not been collected and put in circulation as a group among the churches. They had not been published. Of course Paul had not published them, nor thought of their ever being published. He wrote them each for some definite, immediate purpose, beyond which he did not expect them to go. But they were of such evident religious and practical value that the churches to which he wrote them in many cases kept them and probably read them from time to time in their meetings. The knowledge that such letters existed by ones or twos here and there in the church chests of cities like Philippi, Corinth, or Rome must have been vaguely familiar to traveled Christians, but no one had ever thought to search them out and collect them for general use. Paul had not collected his letters; he had scattered them over Asia Minor and Greece. He had not published them; he had buried them, in obscure, uncultivated groups of Greek Christians. They had fallen into the soil and practically disappeared. This is the explanation of the silence of Acts about them.

The Acts of the Apostles with its striking picture of Paul and his colossal service to Greek Christianity at once put a new face on the matter. It gave to these scattered remains of Paul's writing a new interest and importance and suggested to someone who knew that actual letters of Paul still existed the collecting and publication of them. The proof of this lies in the fact that whereas Acts is silent about Paul's letter-writing the Christian writings that followed Acts are full of signs that a collection of Paul's letters was in circulation, and was making an extraordinary impression.

One of the first Christian books to appear after Acts was the Revelation of John. It actually begins with a collection of letters to seven churches[1]—not at all a natural thing to send to each church of the seven, unless some such letter collection as that of Paul were already in circulation. The more one reflects on the sending to Ephesus, for example, of letters addressed to other churches, the stranger it appears, until we view it in the light of a previously published collection of Paul's letters to churches, which immediately makes it natural and proper. It is all the more surprising at the beginning of an apocalypse or revelation, a kind of writing differing sharply from the personal letter. But this again becomes intelligible when it is seen as the sequel to the publication probably at Ephesus of the first collection of the letters of Paul, and the profound impression it must have produced.

The publication of a collection of Paul's letters to churches had so impressed John that he adopted the letter collection as the form for the portal of his revelation. This fact is the most striking possible proof of the recent appearance of the Pauline collection and of the great impression it had made. It had the extraordinary effect of making the Revelation of John a hybrid literary type, part apocalypse and part collection of letters—a fact that has received little attention and has never been explained. John does not collect his letters to the seven churches; he actually writes the collection—the clearest proof that a collection of Christian letters to churches already existed. This places the making of the Pauline collection with great definiteness. It was made after the publication of Acts and before the writing of the Revelation of John.

Other signs of the impression made by it are not wanting. The use of letters of considerable length as means of Christian instruction at once began to become general. Hebrews, I Peter, and the Letter of Clement of Rome to the Corinthians are the first fruits of this new movement that have come down to us, and fifteen or twenty years later the letters of Ignatius and Polycarp expressly mention Paul's letters as patterns of what they were trying to do. Beginning with Clement, in fact, mentions of Paul as a writer of letters are frequent in this early literature. This is in part the explanation of the old idea that Paul wrote Hebrews; it was written under the influence of the newly published collection of Paul's letters and therefore had a certain broad resemblance to the Pauline letter type. I Peter, too, shows the influence of Paul's letters. This revival of the religious use of letters to churches which Paul had originated was occasioned by the publication of the first collection of his letters, which would naturally have just this effect.

Not less striking is the prompt collecting of the letters of Ignatius of Antioch, who suffered martyrdom at Rome between 107 and 117 A.D.[2] Even before definite news of his martyrdom had reached the east from Rome, the churches of Smyrna and Philippi had begun to collect the letters written during the last months of his life when he was on his way from Antioch to his martyrdom at Rome.[3] In this undertaking the influence of an already existing collection of the letters of that earlier and greater martyr, the apostle Paul, is unmistakable.

In the case of Paul it was done for a man whose figure had come to assume heroic proportions because of the value time had shown his work to possess. In the Revelation of John the letters had no separate existence; they were written simply to form the collection. In the case of Ignatius, his admirers did not even wait for news of his death, in their haste to assemble his letters into a collection. Of these three earliest letter collections thus formed, there can hardly be a moment's doubt which is the first in time as in importance.

The existence of a Pauline collection is therefore the key to the new letter-writing movement of the end of the first and beginning of the second centuries, and to the collections of letters which meet us under the names of John and of Ignatius in the same period. Letter-writing was of course common among Greeks in those times, but not such letter-writing as this. The letter of Christian instruction was in fact almost as distinctive a Christian contribution to literary types as the written gospel. But it was not the writing of Paul's letters but their subsequent collection and publication that brought home to Christian leaders the great possibilities of this form of Christian expression. The letters of Paul had lain like a mine just beneath the feet of the early church, with here and there outcroppings sporadically worked, the whole awaiting the vision and energy of some church or individual to develop its possibilities of worth.

Collections of the letters of notable men were familiar among the Greeks. Plato's letters are often quoted by Cicero and Plutarch, and a

collection of thirteen of them, few of them probably genuine, has come down to us.[4] The letters
of Epicurus (342–270 B.C.) were well known to
followers of his school like Philodemus in the
first century before Christ. The letters of Apollonius of Tyana, a contemporary of the author
of Acts, were collected by the time of Hadrian,
for there is said to have been a collection of them
in his palace at Antium.[5]

The makers of the Pauline collection may
have known the Plato and Epicurus collections.
But after all they were but partial precedents
for their collection, for it was made up of letters
not to individuals but to churches. In this lies
its striking coincidence with the collections of
John and Ignatius afterward. It is not a matter
of letters, but of collections of letters; and further not simply of collections of letters, but of
collections of letters to churches. Clement, Ignatius, and Polycarp can now confidently appeal
to these letters as in the possession of distant
churches, and familiar to them.[6] They were not
simply collected therefore but published.

We can form a fair idea of the size of this
collection. The letter collections of John and of
Ignatius contained seven letters each, and about
a century later the writer of the so-called Mura-

torian list, at Rome, observed that Paul, like John, wrote to seven churches. The collection in its earliest form probably contained seven letters to churches, for once formed it would have been difficult for a letter to a new church unknown to the original collection to gain admittance to it. The earliest writers who refer to Paul's letters among them show acquaintance with at least five letters.[7] The earliest of them, Clement of Rome, is clearly unacquainted with II Corinthians,[8] and that letter was probably absent from the collection in its earliest form but was added to it early in its history. Marcion's list of 140–50 numbered ten letters, and the collection had probably reached that size long before his time, or within a few years of its first appearance. That the letters to Timothy and Titus were part of it in its early stages is unlikely. They came into it after the middle of the second century, increasing it to thirteen—just the number of the letters in the Plato collection.

It is a striking fact that the letter collections of both John and Ignatius begin with a letter to the Ephesians.[9] Marcion's list, about 140, began with Galatians; the Muratorian list, about 200, with Corinthians followed by Ephesians.[10] Ephesians certainly had a more prominent place

in the original collection than it has today. It
may even have begun it. Ephesians was written
in the latter part of the first century, not to any
single church but as a general letter. It shows
the influence of Colossians and must have been
written in connection with the movement to collect Paul's letters, probably as an introduction
to them. The seven letters in the Revelation are
preceded by an introductory letter to all seven
churches, which suggests that at the beginning
of the earlier Pauline collection there was a general introductory letter. The character and contents of Ephesians are decidedly favorable to
this view. It was originally addressed to all
Christians. Ephesus is not mentioned in the letter, according to the oldest manuscripts,[11] and
Marcion a half-century later called it Laodiceans, supposing it to be the letter mentioned
at the end of Colossians. If the collection was
issued from Ephesus, this introductory letter
would very naturally come to be known as
Ephesians. Certainly Ephesians was an important feature of the Pauline collection in its
earliest form.

In writing to the Ephesians about 107–17,
Ignatius says that Paul in every letter remem-
bers or recalls them[12]—a remark of some diffi-

culty, since some of Paul's best-known letters say nothing about Ephesus. What Ignatius probably means is that in view of the Ephesians' connection with the publication of Paul's letters, every such letter brings them to the readers' mind. Certainly almost everything points to Ephesus as the place of origin of the collection. There Paul had worked longest and most successfully. There in all probability Acts was put forth. There Phoebe's letter of introduction to Ephesus, now attached to Romans, would naturally be found.[13] There news of what Pauline letters might survive in the Christian centers of Galatia to the east, Macedonia to the north, Greece to the west, and of course Asia itself would most naturally come. And there the new book, a collection of Christian letters, would most naturally find its first reflection, in the letter collection of the Revelation of John.

The order of the first collection we can only guess. Like the letter collections of John and Ignatius that followed it, it probably began with Ephesians. For the rest, it is more likely to be faithfully reflected in the Muratorian list of 200 than in that of Marcion, and if so, the whole would have run Ephesians (serving as an introduction addressed to Christians generally),

Corinthians (I), Philippians, Colossians, Galatians, Thessalonians (I and II), Romans. Philemon may have stood as a separate letter, but was more probably attached to Colossians, since the seven-fold character of the list in its early form seems to have been an outstanding feature of it.

It is impossible to publish a collection of anyone's letters without editorial work of some kind. Paul did not name his letters, and the several titles, "To Galatians," "To Philippians," and the like, these Ephesian editors must have supplied, usually on the basis of information contained in the salutations of the letters themselves. That they found any considerable number of Paul's letters in existence and made a selection from them is unlikely; more probably they assembled and published all that they could find. The only exception would be II Corinthians, which gave so painful a picture of both Paul and the Corinthians that we are not surprised to find it unknown to I Clement and so probably absent from the earliest form of the collection. It may have been the strong approval with which Clement in his letter to Corinth appeals to I Corinthians[6] that led the Corinthians to bring out of their church chest the rest of their correspondence with Paul, combining his third and fourth letters to them into what we know as II Corinthians. The collection may thus have passed very soon into a second edition at Corinth through the addition of II Corinthians. It was perhaps then that Ephesians and Corinthians exchanged places and the order became that of the later Muratorian list, beginning Corinthians-Ephesians.

The Ephesian editors may have combined two letters to Philippi into our Philippians[14] and added the short letter introducing Phoebe to the church at Ephesus to the great letter to the Romans—a thing all the more likely if Romans stood at the end of the collection. For the purpose of the collection was not historical but practical. The gospel literature, already at its height, was showing the value of Christian writings for the life of the churches, and the religious usefulness of some of Paul's letters had probably never been wholly lost sight of. The Ephesian editors simply introduced the whole surviving body of his letters to the general Christian public, to serve the practical uses of religious life, both public and private. The figures of the apostles were beginning to assume heroic stature in the literature of the time

—Acts, Revelation, I Clement—and especial value would obviously attach to the letters of one so eminent among them as Acts had just shown Paul to be. The letters at once established themselves in the regard of the churches as a great religious message from the beginning of the Greek mission, and from the hero of that movement. They were not yet conceived as scripture or consciously co-ordinated with the writings of the Jewish Bible, but they yet won a peculiar esteem as the work of an apostle.

The service done to Christian literature and life by the men who, probably at Ephesus not far from the year 90 A.D.,[15] collected and published Paul's letters, was immeasurable. They gave to the early churches religious materials of the utmost practical worth and greatly stimulated Christian literary expression. They preserved priceless memorials of the great pioneer missionary to the Greeks which were at the same time historical documents of the highest value for Christian origins. And, without knowing it, they laid the foundation of the New Testament.

THE FIRST COLLECTIONS: THE
FOURFOLD GOSPEL

THE earliest gospel was unwritten. It arose
in that Jewish atmosphere in which the
pious course was not to write and read but to
compose and memorize. Jewish ways of treating the interpretation of the Law affected their
first treatment of their memories of Jesus, whose
sayings early Jewish Christians naturally preserved as they did those of their great rabbis,
in memoriter form.[1]

This practice, which seems so strange to us,
gave rise to the oral gospel. It is clearly reflected in Paul's First Letter to the Corinthians,
chapters 11 and 15, where he refers to parts of
it as received by him and passed on to them; that
is, as tradition. This oral tradition was the gospel of early Jewish Christianity, and, during
Paul's life at least, that of his Greek converts,
to whom he would, as in duty bound, teach it
as soon as they accepted the gospel. We have
glimpses of it not only in Paul but in Acts,[2] in
Clement of Rome, and in Polycarp of Smyrna,

107–17.[3] It was still the prevailing form of the gospel in the early years of the second century.

Under its shadow there sprang up here and there in the Greek world local written gospels, called forth by special circumstances. The first of these, the Gospel of Mark, was written at Rome, perhaps primarily to preserve Peter's recollections of Jesus from being forgotten. It was probably not intended to displace the oral gospel, but simply to supplement it. This was the beginning of the gospel-making movement. Mark became the basis of the Gospel of Matthew, written at Antioch[4] probably soon after 80, and was again used perhaps ten years later by Luke, who wrote a history of the Greek mission in the two volumes known to us as Luke and Acts. This was done probably at Ephesus. Other local gospels were the Gospel according to the Hebrews and the Gospel according to the Egyptians, which were current in Egypt by the middle of the second century. These local gospels are to be thought of not as substitutes for the oral gospel but as supplements to it, which Greek Christianity especially, with its fondness for written books, would require. Each of these had its own circle of readers, who doubtless used it in conjunction with the old established oral gospel.

Early in the second century when it was becoming plain that the public of Christianity lay in the Greek world, there was written at Ephesus a new gospel which undertook to transplant Christianity into Greek soil, and translate its message into Greek terms. This was the Gospel of John. It must have made a great impression, and naturally seemed to challenge not so much the old oral gospel as the newer written forms of the gospel such as those of Mark at Rome, Matthew at Antioch, and Luke at Ephesus. These books, or at least Matthew and Luke, with their more Jewish ways of presenting Christianity, must have been brought forward by conservative people opposed to the new gospel, and come into competition with it. And this led, a few years after the appearance of the Gospel of John, to its combination with its rival local gospels to form the fourfold gospel.

The earliest order of the collection was probably just that familiar to us today: Matthew, Mark, Luke, John.[5] It thus began with the most Jewish of the gospels, and ended with the most Greek, being intended to be read through, from beginning to end, and to close with the new

Greek recast of the Christian message, from which it justly hoped great things. The four-fold gospel was meant to win a wider hearing for the Gospel of John than it would by itself receive, and it had just that result. In making it, its framers had no thought of offering to the Christian public a collection of inspired scripture, still less of beginning a New Testament to be a companion to the Jewish Bible. Their aim was rather to bring the Gospel of John before Greek Christians everywhere, in such a way as to conciliate those who were already attached to earlier and more Jewish gospels and commend the new gospel most effectively to them.

We are not to suppose that Christians at the beginning of the second century welcomed a variety of written gospels. They were much more inclined to accept one in preference to all others. To accept two would at once raise historical and liturgical questions about matters on which they disagreed. And it was by putting forward the new collection as a unit—the Gospel: according to Matthew, according to Mark, according to Luke, according to John—that this aversion to many gospels was met. This was in effect an admission on the part of its framers that however much John might seem to differ from the earlier gospels, it was still the old gospel message which they loved that it presented. For in putting John on an equality with Matthew, Mark, and Luke in the new collection, its makers were also putting them on the same footing with John, and giving them a recognition which their adherents would appreciate.

So while we find Paul, Clement, and Polycarp using the oral gospel; Matthew and Luke using Mark; Ignatius, Barnabas, and the Teaching of the Twelve Apostles[6] using Matthew; and Marcion using Luke, most of the books written toward the middle of the second century or soon after it show acquaintance with the fourfold gospel. The Preaching of Peter, II Peter, the Gospel of Peter, Papias of Hierapolis, the recently found Epistle of the Apostles, and Justin Martyr, all know the fourfold gospel. Justin wrote at Rome after 150, but he became a Christian at Ephesus as early as 135, and probably there became attached to the new fourfold gospel. The fact that the Ephesian Gospel of John was probably from the point of view of those who made the collection the germ and kernel of it also strongly confirms the impression that it was made at Ephesus. If the motive of the makers of the fourfold gospel was to extend the influence of the Gospel of John, certainly in no other place is it so likely to have been made as in Ephesus, where the Gospel of John was written. If Ephesus had already witnessed the making of the first collection of Paul's letters, it would be most natural that the first collection of gospels should be made there. Its use by Papias of Hierapolis, a city within a hundred miles of Ephesus, points in the same direction. On the other hand Hermas of Rome writing between 125 and 150 is unacquainted with it, and so it cannot have originated there.

At Ephesus, then, in all probability, and about 125, for Justin seems to have found it there ten years later, the fourfold gospel was put forth. It contained the Gospel of Matthew, which was probably written at Antioch; the Roman Gospel of Mark, which had already lost its ending, and was accordingly supplied with a conclusion based for the most part upon Luke; the Gospel of Luke, which was now necessarily separated from its companion volume, Acts, and took the name of a gospel; and the new Gospel of John, to which an epilogue, chapter 21, was added, recognizing more fully than the gospel itself had previously done the place of Peter, indorsing the message of the new gospel, and commending it and the whole collection to the churches in a sentence which is really the Finis to the fourfold gospel: "There are many other things that Jesus did, so many in fact that if they were all written out, I do not suppose that the world itself would hold the books that would have to be written."[7]

The four gospels were not collected and put forth together as authorities, but they were not long in coming to be so regarded. The authority which of course attached to the numerous sayings of Jesus that they contained naturally extended to the gospels that contained these sayings, and within twenty-five years of their publication these "Memoirs of the Apostles" were being read in Christian meetings side by side with the Greek translation of the Jewish Bible.

Other books were indeed appearing which made larger claims than these. The Teaching of the Lord through the Twelve Apostles to the Heathen was based (about 150) upon a little work probably of the same name half a century older.[8] In both forms of it we see the early church feeling after an authoritative formulation of what it regarded as apostolic teaching, probably in contrast to Paul's, in an age when it was still free from any such written authority. The same freedom marks the Roman apocalypse of Hermas called the "Shepherd."[9] It consists not only of visions but of a new series of twelve commandments and a group of ten parables. In the thought of Matthew and Barnabas, Jesus was the new lawgiver,[10] and we instinctively think of the parable as his characteristic form of teaching. Yet this Roman prophet toward 150 thinks himself qualified by inspiration to give both commandments and parables to all the churches. Nor did the churches resent this as presumption on his part. They welcomed his work, which enjoyed a wide popularity and even found its way into many early New Testaments.

But none of these seriously rivaled the fourfold gospel. It contained the earliest gospels of which we have any knowledge, which represented the chief centers of Christianity north of the Mediterranean. These books were rich in religious instruction and inspiration, and their variety adapted them to any circle. Their simple narrative form, with its moving story of Jesus and his heroic ministry, made an extraordinary appeal. The individual local gospels could not stand before them, and when half a century after their first collection, the New Testament came into being, their inclusion in it was a foregone conclusion. They had become a unit and there was no thought of choosing between them. Without them it was unthinkable and the fourfold gospel became its cornerstone.

V

THE FIRST CHRISTIAN
SCRIPTURE

THE vague and informal authority with which some Christian writings were being credited began about the middle of the second century to give way to something more rigid and definite. This was due to the activity of one man, Marcion. He was a native of Sinope, in Pontus, a shipowner and a man of wealth. He felt that Christianity had been Judaized and was in need of reformation, and he undertook to bring it back to the views of Paul.[1] About 140 he visited Rome, and there he met the Gnostic Cerdo, who influenced his thinking. Marcion gave money to the Roman church, and tried to enlist it in his campaign to free Christianity from Jewish trammels and bring it back to what he believed to be the ideas of Christ and Paul. In this he failed, and in 144 he withdrew from the church and began to organize his followers into a church of his own. To this work he devoted the remaining twenty years of his life, with much success.

Marcion had come to the conviction that the God of wrath and justice depicted in the Jewish scriptures could not be identical with the loving Father revealed in Jesus. He accordingly recognized in the Jewish God the Creator, the just God of Nature, and in the Father of Jesus a superior being, the good God of Redemption. With these views it was clearly impossible for him to retain the high esteem for the Jewish scriptures which had prevailed in the churches from the first. But these had so established themselves in Christian worship and devotion that it was impossible to dislodge them, at least without putting something in their place. Here the genius of Marcion showed itself. He proposed to replace the Jewish scriptures with a Christian collection consisting of Gospel and Apostle, as the Jewish did of Law and Prophets. The gospel was the one we know as Luke's; the apostle was Paul, ten of whose letters made up this second part of the collection. Marcion accompanied these with a work of his own called the Antitheses, in which he sought to show the contradictions between the Jewish scriptures and Christian teaching, and this book probably formed part of the new collection of scripture on which he sought to unite the Christian churches.

For Marcion's aim was to bring all the churches to his way of thinking and not to divide but to unite them on a higher platform. He was right in thinking that Jewish ways of conceiving religion were insensibly pervading Christian circles, and that the great ideas of faith and freedom for which Paul had stood were being lost. The pastoral letters and the Teaching of the Twelve Apostles show how formality was creeping into church life. Marcion had no historical conception of religious development which would enable him to relate the ideas of God in the Jewish scriptures with the loftier teachings of Jesus, and the only way he saw to escape the encroachments of Jewish theology and practice was to break with the Jewish scriptures altogether.

Marcion contended that Paul had rightly interpreted the gospel, and he meant to recall the Christian movement to Pauline views. Like Paul, Marcion laid emphasis upon faith and thus distinguished himself from the great Gnostic thinkers of his day with whom his fantastic theological ideas ally him. Yet he was no real Paulinist. As Harnack has said, Marcion was the only man in the second century who really tried to understand Paul, and he misunderstood him.

Marcion's movement met with extraordinary success. Justin, who is the first writer to mention him, says that in every race of men he has won many to his views.[2] Irenaeus says that he mutilated the Gospel of Luke and dismembered the letters of Paul in the interests of his views, and Tertullian goes over his text almost verse by verse to show just what he left out.[3] His treatment of the text was no doubt controlled in part by the views he wished to propagate, for example, his omission of Luke's account of Jesus' birth. But it must be recognized that his correction of the text was also in part honest and sound.

Marcion's Christian scripture of course seemed very defective to the writers of the first and second generations after him. But his contemporary Justin does not urge this point against him. The books of Marcion's scripture as reported by Tertullian were the gospel known to us as Luke's and ten letters of Paul: Galatians, I and II Corinthians, Romans, I and II Thessalonians, Laodiceans (that is, Ephesians), Colossians, Philippians, and Philemon. Marcion naturally put Galatians first as Paul's most vigorous pronouncement against the Judaizers.[4]

Marcion stands out in the history of canon

formation as the the first man who can be identi-
fied as definitely setting out to form a Christian
scripture. On the other hand, he could not have
met with such success if the books he chose were
not already highly and even reverently esteemed
by the churches. We have seen how the words
of Jesus and the teachings of the apostles had
come to be recognized as authoritative in Christian circles, and books embodying them were
being read in Christian meetings side by side
with the Law and the Prophets. The leading
letters of Paul had long since been gathered into
a collection and published among the churches,
and the fourfold gospel was already in church
use. These conditions made it easy to accept
Marcion's Christian scripture, which did hardly
more than define and regulate what was already
the practice of many churches. But the churches
in general could not be prevailed upon to give up
the Jewish scripture, and in his effort to secure
this Marcion failed, though Marcionite churches
long continued to exist.[5]

Later writers, reading back into Marcion's
time the conditions of their own, condemned
him for omitting from his collection of authoritative documents books which after his time
came to be considered canonical. From one

point of view this criticism as applied to certain books was just. Marcion clearly selected from among the gospels current in his day the one most nearly suited to his extreme Paulinism. The collection of four gospels was probably well known to him, and while it was already becoming popular among the churches it was not yet thought of as canonical scripture. Over against the Law and Prophets of the old scripture Marcion proposed to set the Gospel and the Apostle, or the Lord and the Apostle. This gave him room, as he conceived it, for but one gospel, and Luke came nearest to meeting his doctrinal requirements. If he knew it in its original position as part of a two-volume work, with the Acts as the second part—and with his great admiration for Paul, he must have known Acts in some form—it is easy to see why he omitted Acts from his new Christian scripture, for it reconciled Paul with Judaistic Christianity in a way Marcion could not have tolerated.

We are not to think of Marcion as the first man to collect and publish Paul's letters; that, as we have seen, was done long before his day. He did not even separate the Gospel of Luke from its companion volume known to us as the Acts of the Apostles; that, too, had been effected

by the makers of the fourfold gospel. What he
actually did was to conceive the idea of combining a representative gospel with the well-
known collection of Paul's letters, and giving the
whole the authority of Christian scripture. The
thought that Christianity should have its own
scripture collection originated with Marcion. It
was his contribution to the formation of the New
Testament. The main structure of the New Testament that was to be was also foreshadowed by
Marcion when he made his collection consist of
Gospel and Apostle.

But the chief significance of Marcion lay in
his masterful idea that if the scattered and di-
verse churches were to be effectively united
against the foes that threatened them from
within and from without, they must determine
upon an authoritative platform, and that the
best materials for that platform were the ancient
documents already familiar and highly prized
among the churches, which used them along with
the Jewish scriptures and various other Christian writings, in their Sunday meetings. The
principal thing in his position that would be felt
as an innovation was his displacement of the
Jewish Bible and of various other books which
churches were accustomed to hear read in their

meetings. This is in part the reason why Marcion was regarded by later writers as a reducer of Christian scripture, not the first framer of it.

In writing his letters to his churches Paul had done much to make them known to, and interested in, one another. The writer of Ephesians had declared his vision of the union of the churches in Christ. The publication of Paul's letters, including Ephesians, was a long step toward unification. The Gospel of John makes an eloquent appeal for unity, and its republication as part of the fourfold gospel, representing Antioch, Ephesus, and Rome, was another step in that direction. Twenty-five years later Marcion saw the perils of the scattered churches, and sought to unify and organize them into a great comprehensive church. Later writers thought of him as a schismatic, but it was his conception of an organized Christianity with a scripture, Gospel and Apostle, of its own, that afterward found successful expression in the Catholic church.

THE AGE OF JUSTIN

IN THE middle of the second century, the Christians of Rome would gather on Sunday and listen to the reading of the Memoirs of the Apostles or the Writings of the Prophets. This is the statement of Justin, who was a member of the Roman church at that time.[1] Justin was born in Palestine, at Flavia Neapolis, the modern Nablus. He made some study of Greek philosophy, and probably at Ephesus, toward the year 135, he became a Christian. About 140 he became a Christian teacher, and a few years later went to Rome, where Marcion was already established. By the time Justin reached Rome, Marcion, who had come under the influence of Cerdo, had left the church and begun the organization of churches of his peculiar Pauline type. With men at Rome like Valentinus, Cerdo, Marcion, Justin, and Tatian, the years that followed were of great significance there.

At Rome Justin wrote the only books of his that have come down to us, an Apology and a Dialogue. The Apology is addressed to the emperor Antoninus and undertakes to defend the Christians against the charges of atheism and disloyalty commonly made against them, and to show the affinities of Christianity with true philosophy. It was written soon after 150. In the Dialogue, written a few years later, Justin points out the fulfilment in Christianity of the inspired utterances of the Jewish prophets, and argues from these to the truth of Christianity.

Justin quotes from the Old Testament more than seven hundred times. Some of these quotations are mere passing reminiscences of its language, but in some cases, on the other hand, he quotes an entire psalm, or a whole page from the prophets. His quotations are from the Septuagint Greek version of the Jewish scriptures, which he goes so far as to claim for the Christian church. "These words," he says to Trypho, his Jewish opponent in the Dialogue, "are in your scriptures, or rather not yours, but ours. For we believe them, but you when you read them do not perceive the meaning that is in them."[2] This long and elaborate argument of Justin's was part of the violent controversy caused by Marcion's rejection of the Jewish scriptures. It was a great counterblast to Marcion's Antitheses. Marcion maintained that Christianity contradicted the Jewish scriptures; Justin maintained that it fulfilled them.

By the Writings of the Prophets, Justin evidently meant the books of what we call the Old Testament, although his list of them would probably include some of those now called Apocrypha. But what were the Memoirs of the Apostles which he says were read before the preaching and the prayers in these early Roman meetings? He himself explains that these Memoirs were called "gospels,"[3] and that they were composed by the apostles and those who followed them.[4] He sometimes speaks of them collectively as "the gospel," and refers to sayings recorded in the gospel, very much as we do. He never mentions any evangelist by name, but once says that the change of Peter's name is recorded "in his memoirs,"[5] as though one gospel or book of memoirs bore the name of Peter.

But while Justin does not name the gospels that were read at Rome in his day, his use of them in his writings leaves us under no uncertainty as to what they were. The gospels of Matthew, Mark, Luke, and John were the ones which he used, and described as the Memoirs composed by the apostles and those who followed them. By the Memoirs of Peter he probably meant the Gospel of Mark, for which Papias and the writer of II Peter[6] in Justin's day, and many writers afterward, considered Peter to be the chief authority. Justin uses Matthew most, and Mark and John least. It is true that he quotes John's phraseology decidedly less than that of the others, but the influence upon him of John's principal ideas, such as the Logos and the incarnation, is very marked. He may have known of other gospels such as that of Peter, but his use of them is too slight to compare with his use even of Mark or John. It is evident that these four gospels stand with him on the same general level and that although he may have known and even used other gospels, they did not, in his mind, equal these four in worth and standing. In fact, he was not so familiar with them as he was with the four we know in our New Testament.

The Memoirs of the Apostles which were read in church in Rome in Justin's day therefore were the gospels of Matthew, Mark, Luke, and John. This is all the more striking when we remember that Hermas, writing at Rome a few years before, shows no acquaintance with the four gospels and little if any with any one of them. The four gospels must have come into this position of pre-eminence at Rome toward the middle of the century, under the influence of men like Justin from the neighborhood of Ephesus where, as we have seen, the collection of them into one group was probably made. It is, moreover, in striking contrast with the movement previously begun by Marcion to establish the Gospel of Luke as the one authoritative gospel. Marcion was at work in Rome seeking to bring the churches to his way of thinking, but his effort to put Luke in the place of the fourfold gospel did not convince the Roman church of Justin's day. Perhaps it came too late, and found the four gospels already too well intrenched in the affection and practice of the churches.

Not that the gospels were as yet definitely regarded as inspired. Justin does not so describe them. And yet the fact that they were being read in church along with the Writings of the Prophets shows that in Rome they already outranked other gospels and were on the way to being thought of as sacred scripture like the books of the Old Testament. Justin himself in his later work, the Dialogue, sometimes quotes them with the words "it is written," just as he does the Old Testament.

Justin knew the Revelation of John. It is, in fact, the one book of our New Testament which he calls by name. It was "a Revelation," he declares, "made to a man named John, one of the apostles of Christ."[7] This is the first mention of the Revelation in Christian literature, and comes from one whose early Christian life was spent at Ephesus, in the vicinity of which the Revelation was written. Justin is well acquainted with the book, and identifies its author with the apostle John, but it has left no such impression on his pages as the Gospel of John did. He had probably first read it at Ephesus in his early Christian life there, along with the four gospels.

What place had the letters of Paul in the thought of Justin? It is a singular fact that although his extant works are about equal in extent to the four gospels combined, he nowhere mentions the name of Paul, nor any of his letters. And yet he knows many of them. His evident use of Romans, I Corinthians, Galatians, Ephesians, and Colossians, and his apparent acquaintance with others make it clear that Justin had a collection of Paul's letters as large as that which Marcion was championing.

The silence of Justin as to Paul is very per-

plexing. It must be remembered that we have
only Justin's apologetic works; all his other writings have been lost, and in them he may have
said much about Paul and his letters. But the
probability is that Justin's hesitation to say
much about Paul is due to the extreme emphasis
that Marcion and his followers were just then
putting upon him. Marcion had adopted Paul,
and to make much of Paul in the middle of the
second century seemed like supporting Marcion
and his views, which was the last thing Justin
wished to do. Besides he found the thought of
John much more congenial than that of Paul.

Marcion's zealous campaign on behalf of
Paul's letters thus had the effect of putting them
under a cloud with many Christians in the middle years of the second century. II Peter reflects this, though in a different way. Its writer
knows the collection of Paul's letters, and even
considers them as scripture, but when he refers
to them by name, he is careful to disclaim any
sympathy with those ignorant and unsteadfast
people who were twisting them and the rest of
the scriptures to their own ruin.[8] It is evident
that in Marcion's time those who used Paul's
letters felt that they must either refrain from
mentioning his name or be careful not to have

their interest in Paul taken to mean attachment to his self-appointed champion Marcion.

Both Justin and the writer of II Peter knew a collection of Paul's letters, as well as the group of four gospels. But Justin does not think of Paul's letters as on an equality with the four gospels. They were not read in church with the Writings of the Prophets.

Justin was familiar with Hebrews, though he does not mention it by that or any other name. Hebrews left a marked impression upon the Roman church, and all the early writings of Rome after its appearance reflect its use. But neither Justin nor anyone else in Rome in the second century seems to have thought of its being scripture. The only Christian book which Justin really thought of as scripture was the Revelation of John. Even the gospels which were being read in church along with the Writings of the Prophets which Justin found fulfilled in them were not yet considered scripture like the prophets. But the public reading of them in church shows that they were on their way to becoming scriptural authority.

Justin's pupil Tatian came to Rome from the east soon after Justin, and after Justin's death became a missionary among the Syrians about

Edessa. He wrote an Address to the Greeks about the time of Justin's Apology, 150–155, and later, about 172, among the Syrians published his Syriac interweaving of the four gospels, which he called the Diatessaron. In this work he used only the gospels of Matthew, Mark, Luke, and John. It became the recognized form of the gospel among the Syrians and continued to hold that place among them for fully two hundred years. Tatian's use of the four gospels in this very bold rearrangement shows that with him as with Justin they stood on a higher level than any others, but they were not yet considered scripture, and the way in which the Syriac Diatessaron immediately established itself as the gospel in Syria shows that the separate gospels had not yet appeared there in Syriac.[9]

Tatian's Address to the Greeks shows little use of the gospels, and even less of Paul's letters; but he is said to have revised Paul's letters in an effort to improve their style,[10] and also to have included Titus among them. Like Justin he evidently knew them but did not consider them of equal value with the four gospels. The age of Justin witnessed the rise of the fourfold gospel to a place in Christian worship side by side with the inspired writings of the Jewish prophets.

VII

ON THE THRESHOLD OF THE NEW TESTAMENT

THE church life of the second century was overshadowed by four great heretical movements. The opening years of the century were clouded by Docetism; the middle years by the activities of Marcion and of the Gnostics—followers of Basilides and Valentinus; and the closing years by the Montanists. Reaction against these tendencies found a curious expression in the later years of the century in the appearance in Asia Minor of groups of Christians afterward called Alogi from their aversion to the Logos doctrine of the Gospel of John. They were opposed to John because they felt that its Logos doctrine left too much room for Docetism and because its doctrine of the Paraclete or Comforter seemed to give color to the claims of the Montanists that they were inspired by the Holy Spirit. Montanus actually claimed to be the Paraclete. The Alogi went so far as to declare that the Gospel of John was really the work of Cerinthus, a leading Docetist of the time. Yet

the Alogi did not seem to their Christian contemporaries to be unorthodox because of these
views, and this shows how loosely the gospel
canon was still held in Asia Minor even after
the middle of the second century.

But most Christians of the time accepted the
fourfold gospel. Athenagoras of Athens writing
about 177 A.D. makes use of it, and of the letters
of Paul, in his Plea for the Christians and his
work On the Resurrection. Yet he does not mention Paul or any of the evangelists by name,
though he once quotes a phrase of I Corinthians
as from "the apostle."[1] The cloud which had for
a time in the middle of the second century rested
upon Paul on account of Marcion's adoption
and advocacy of his letters evidently lifted as
the years passed. Athenagoras' way of introducing his occasional gospel quotations with "it
says" by its very naturalness shows how instinctively he relied upon the gospels. It is
Athenagoras who speaks of the Holy Spirit as
making use of the prophets "as a flute-player
breathes into a flute."[2] So mechanical was his
view of inspiration.

The prophets, the gospel, and the apostle are
clearly familiar Christian authorities for Athenagoras, but it is in the prophets that he most

definitely recognizes inspiration. The gospels and the letters of Paul, while used by him with equal confidence, are not yet a recognized part of his inspired scriptures. Their relation to such a scripture is still informal.

Between 180 and 190 Theophilus, bishop of Antioch, wrote a number of books, among them, it is said, a commentary on a gospel harmony; but of these only his defense of Christianity, in three books addressed to his friend Autolycus, has been preserved. Theophilus had the greatest reverence for the Jewish Bible—the Holy Scriptures, as he often calls it.[3] He also had a high respect for the gospels; once he definitely coordinates them with the Law and the Prophets, "because they all spoke inspired by one spirit of God."[4] The Sibyl, the prophetess of the Greeks, Theophilus held, also spoke under divine inspiration;[5] indeed, he quotes the Sibylline oracles then current at great length and with full approval. But neither they nor the gospels probably belonged to what he called the Holy Scriptures. This work of Theophilus contains the first explicit quotation of one of the gospels that has come down to us.[6] It is from the Gospel of John, whom it describes as inspired. It speaks of his gospel in the same breath with the Holy Scriptures, but not as though it belonged to them. The situation in Theophilus is very curious. It is evidently transitional. The Holy Scriptures is the name of a very definite group of books. The gospels do not belong to this group. Yet they are inspired, just as the Holy Scriptures are.

Theophilus knows a number of the letters of Paul, and once refers to them as utterances of "the divine word." At Antioch, then, in Theophilus' day, the Holy Scriptures of the Jews are still pre-eminent; but the four gospels and the letters of Paul are also inspired, and of these the gospels still stand on a higher level than the letters. But both are just coming into an esteem virtually equal to that of the Holy Scriptures.

With Theophilus, we are in short on the very threshold of New Testament.

In July, 180 A.D., certain Christians of the town of Scili in North Africa were examined by the governor before their execution. On being asked what they had in their church chest, they answered, "The books and the letters of Paul, a righteous man." The language is very vague, but in the light of the usage of the time, as we have seen it reflected in Theophilus and Athenagoras, we can hardly doubt that their "books" were the prophets and the gospels. The letters of Paul, although kept with them in the church chest, did not as yet equal them in sanctity. At Scili the gospels had come to be thought of as a regular part of their most sacred books. They already belonged to their Bible, as we should say, and as they actually did say, when they used Greek, for their word for books was *Bibloi* or *Biblia*, and it is from just this use of the word, to mean *the* Books par excellence, that our word "Bible" comes.

So the martyrs of Scili were already thinking of the gospels as part of the Bible, but not of Paul's letters as belonging to it, although they too were kept in the church chest and read occasionally in public worship.

Between 170 and 180 A.D. Melito of Sardis addressed his defense of the Christians to the emperor Marcus Aurelius. He wrote many other books, among others one on the Revelation of John. Melito took part in the controversy with the Montanists, whose excesses and extreme prophetic claims offended so many of his contemporaries.

Much greater interest attaches to Melito's Selections from the Prophets, in the preface to which he gives a list of the books of the Old

Covenant, as he had learned them on a visit to Palestine. His list lacks those characteristic books of the Greek version of the Old Testament which we call the Apocrypha. But what is most striking is his way of describing them as the books of the Old Covenant or Testament. Had men in his day begun to think of an "Old Testament" as a collection of books, and if so must it not have been in contrast to a "New Testament" collection? At any rate, Melito is on the verge of using the Old Testament in a literary sense just as we do, and here again we find ourselves very literally on the threshold of the New Testament.

Even about 180 there is still a surprising variety among Christians as to what books should be considered scripture. Melito omits the Apocrypha from the Jewish scripture. The Alogi do not accept the Gospel of John. Theophilus calls only the Law and the Prophets Holy Scriptures, although he believes the gospels and Paul are equally inspired. The martyrs of Scili include the gospels, but not the letters of Paul, in their Books—the first foreshadowing of the Christian Bible. And Melito of Sardis with his interest in the Revelation, and his researches into just what belonged to

the "Books of the Old Testament," is uncon-
sciously pointing the way to the New. Without
knowing it, the churches were ready for the New
Testament and the Christian Bible. Those con-
ceptions when they came were not wholly new.
It was a short step to them. But it was a step,
and a very definite one. The variety of opinion
that existed made it difficult. Yet everything
was in readiness for it. How did it come to be
taken?

VIII

THE FIRST NEW TESTAMENT

A CENTURY of conflict with the sects had shown the churches the dangers as well as the delights of unrestrained individualism. From the shadowy figures of the Nicolaitans of Revelation to the ecstatic prophets who were so successfully spreading Montanism over the Roman world at the end of the second century, the sects were constantly in the picture. These were primarily groups of devout Christians who became so absorbed by the views of some taking or profound religious leader that they lost touch with the thought and experience of the churches around them and came to be considered extreme and erratic. Capable and earnest men like Cerinthus, Basilides, Valentinus, Cerdo, Marcion, and Montanus had formed the centers of these groups, which stood apart not only from each other but from the general Christianity about them.

Toward the close of the second century this general Christianity began to express and assert itself. Too long it had left the great practical measures of definition, organization, and canonization to the sects. The schismatics had been forward with their claims and their formulations. General Christianity had been slow with such measures. Marcion had sought to organize the church, and had actually proposed a definite Christian scripture in place of the Jewish scripture as a basis of union. But this plan had sacrificed values too real and great for general acceptance. It needed a broader platform and a less rigorous spirit to unite the widespread groups which remained untouched by the erratic tendencies of the day. The extreme prophetic claims of Montanism in particular forced upon the church the more definite fixing of its primitive authorities, under the form of a covenant or Testament too original and sacred to admit of modern amplification.

Such a spirit and purpose found expression somewhere about 180 in the founding of the Catholic, that is the general, or non-sectarian church. In this movement the defects of the earlier latitude and disorganization were remedied. More than one leaf was taken from the book of the thriving sects, and the definition, organization, and canonization which they had found so serviceable were pressed into the service of the general church. If certain vague but precious liberties were sacrificed, some very definite practical gains were secured.

The Catholic movement was not an arbitrary system imposed upon the churches against their will, nor a mere spontaneous and inevitable culmination of forces long since at work. Such forces entered importantly into it, and all the materials of it already existed. One of its striking traits was the recognition of a New Testament collection of scripture of equal authority with the Old. But the books which it gathered into this collection were old and for the most part familiar to the churches. Their canonization meant little more for most churches than the clear recognition and definition of what already vaguely existed. Other men had thought of having a Christian scripture, other men had put the gospels in their Bible, and acknowledged the inspiration of the letters of Paul. The Catholic movement simply pressed this upon all the churches. The office of bishop had long existed in some churches, and the baptismal confession of faith used at Rome had developed in the strife with the sects. To invite the churches in general to accept such a scripture, organization, and creed as a common platform seemed to those who led in it no more than the recognition and regulation of practices already more or less prevalent. Indeed, they might with sincerity think them, in principle at least, as old as Christianity itself, and urge them upon the churches as no novelty but in effect simply a return to apostolic Christianity.

But if the materials of the new structure were many of them old, the consciousness which found expression in it was new and the movement owed its beginning to wise and able ecclesiastical statesmen. Who they were is less clear than where they worked, for our first glimpses of the new movement we catch in the circle of influence of the Church of Rome.

Irenaeus, the bishop of Lyons, about 185 wrote his Refutation of Gnosticism, and a few years later his Proof of the Apostolic Preaching. He looked to Rome as the nearest church of apostolic foundation, and declared that the apostolic character of its views and practices was guaranteed by the fact that its line of bishops could be traced back to apostolic times unbroken; that is, at no time had the control of the church been in the hands of the schismatics.[1] All such churches, Irenaeus held, were in agreement as to what constituted genuine apostolic Christianity, and this agreement proved that they were right.

Tertullian of Carthage, writing his voluminous works toward the end of the second century and after the beginning of the third, held similar views as to the value of the apostolic tradition of the Roman church,[2] although in later life he himself rebelled against the restraints of the new movement and became a Montanist.

A third glimpse of Catholic beginnings is gained from the document called from its Italian discoverer the Muratorian Fragment.[3] It is an actual list of the contents of the New Testament, with reasons for the acceptance of some of its books, and may be the work of that Victor who was bishop of Rome about 200 A.D. and who took it upon himself to excommunicate the Asian bishops who disagreed with him as to the date of Easter. But whether by Victor or not, the Fragment is a Roman work of about that date. From these three writers we gain our first clear impressions of the new movement, especially in its bearings upon the formation of the New Testament scripture.

For the greatest accomplishment of the founders of the Catholic movement was the creation of the New Testament. Not of course in the sense of writing it, but in the sense of assembling and canonizing its several parts, and thus recognizing in them a new authority. While the making of the New Testament was for the most part the recognition of positions already substantially reached though not generally realized, it was more than this. And in this addition to the current authorities of the churches lay probably the chief interest of the canon-makers. In assuming to formulate and define the New Testament they found opportunity to include in it some books that were not in general use among the churches, which especially served the immediate purposes of the new movement.

The movement found its best protection against the innovations of the schismatics in the appeal to the apostles. It would vindicate the truth of its positions by a resort to Christian origins as embodied in them. And ready to its hand lay that collection of the letters of Paul which for nearly a century had been well known among the churches, and had come to pass under the very acceptable name, "the apostle." Partially eclipsed a generation earlier by the undesirable patronage of Marcion, the Pauline collection was now caught back into the very

71

bosom of the church as the base of an apostolic scripture. A few personal letters to Timothy and Titus unknown to Marcion's list and notably favorable to Catholic ideals of organization and practical church life, filled it out to thirteen letters; for Hebrews was not yet accepted at Rome as a work of Paul.

Beside it, and indeed before it, was placed the great quartet of gospels for which more than any others apostolic authors or vouchers could be claimed. Like the letters of Paul, these gospels did not have to be collected. They had already existed for half a century as a collection, and were widely regarded as inspired. It is one of the strange features of the second century that the four gospels resisted the natural tendency to combine them, and continued to circulate collected indeed, but not combined. Tatian had interwoven them for his missionary work in Syria and his work found echoes later in Latin and in other forms, but the four separate gospels were too strongly intrenched in the use and the regard of the churches to lose their individualities in such a blending. Three possibilities lay before the Christian of the second century. He might choose one out of the four and achieve unity by selection, as Marcion did in choosing

Luke, and Valentinus in choosing John. Or he might combine them into one, as Tatian did for his Syrian followers, and Victor of Capua followed him in doing,[4] and as Thomas Jefferson and many other have done in modern times. This was perhaps the most natural course to take, since it was by this method of combination of earlier accounts that the gospels themselves had arisen, and the mental effort of further combination cannot be permanently avoided, if the four are to be historically harmonized.

Fortunately, the non-schismatic churches of the second century took neither of these paths to unification. They felt the need of unity in their gospel but satisfied it by conceiving the collection as a unit. It was the Gospel—according to Matthew, according to Mark, according to Luke, and according to John. These names are probably as old as the collection, for Papias, about 135, already knows them. And it was the fact that back of each of the four parts an apostle was understood to stand as author or at least, for Mark and Luke, as authority, that saved the individuality of the four. The apostolic sanctions were blurred and lost in a harmony like Tatian's, and the controversies of the second century, if nothing else, showed the churches the value of those sanctions. To Justin the gospels were the Memoirs of the Apostles. It was this conception of them that made them resist and survive the strong tendency to amalgamation, and preserved them separate yet collected for the use of the Catholic framers of the first New Testament.

Not, indeed, the first Christian scripture. Marcion had assembled that a generation earlier, and laid down lines that could not be improved. Like his, the new Christian scripture consisted of Gospel and Apostle. But the gospel is no single selected one but the great quartet which had risen to such a point of favor among the churches that it scarcely needed formal adoption as Christian scripture. To go back upon it was, in fact, virtually impossible. It had made its own place in church life and controversy. Most of all in an hour when apostolic authorities were demanded, the fourfold gospel took its place of right at the head of the new scripture. But it was not as four gospels but as one that it did so.

These two great collections, the gospels and the Pauline letters, were bound together by what now came to be known as the Acts of the Apostles. It had probably not gone by that name before. It is not a very accurate description of what it contains. But the rise of Acts of John and Acts of Paul between 160 and 180, and their own fixed purpose of emphasizing apostolic relations, probably suggested to the makers of the new collection the renaming of the second volume of Luke's history the Acts of All the Apostles, as the Muratorian writer calls it. This book, which now emerges from a long period of relative obscurity, supplied a vital link in the new scripture. It filled out still further the rather shadowy figures of the apostles, and showed the relation of Paul to the primitive Christian movement. It thus served to weld together the two collections, to show that Paul was in a real sense an apostle, and thus to make the collection of his letters valid apostolic evidence. It is this bringing forward of Acts to serve as the core of the new scripture that most clearly shows that it was something more than a spontaneous, unconscious process. The gospels and the Pauline letters indeed lay before the makers of the canon ready to their hands, already established in the esteem and affections of the churches, but the new rôle of Acts cannot be thus explained. It had occupied no such position as they.

With it in the new scripture were associated

such letters of apostolic authorship as could be found. What had long before been done for Paul now begins to be done for the other apostles as a group. Irenaeus prized a letter of Peter and one of John, though his Letter of John included what we call II John as well as I John. But to Irenaeus they formed one letter, just as for us Paul's letter introducing Phoebe forms one letter with Romans.

Victor of Rome, the probable author of the Muratorian Fragment, mentions two letters of John and one of Jude, and Tertullian used I Peter, I John, and Jude. This little group forms the beginning of the Catholic or general epistles. The collection of them is one of the two points on which there is most variation in later forms of the New Testament.

The other point of most variation is the revelations. For the first New Testament had not only its collections of gospels, Pauline letters, and letters of other apostles, but a collection of two or even three apocalypses. Irenaeus quoted not only the Revelation of John but the Shepherd of Hermas as scripture. The writer of the Muratorian Fragment accepted the Revelation of John and that of Peter in his New Testament, but admits that some will not have the Revelation of Peter read in church. He condemns the Shepherd, because it was not written by an apostle but recently by their fellow-Christian Hermas, of Rome, and so ought never to be read in church among the prophets, since their number is complete, nor among the apostles. Tertullian uses the Revelation of John, but never mentions that of Peter, and rejects the Shepherd of Hermas with great scorn for the laxity of its moral ideas.[5]

All three therefore accepted the Revelation of John; Irenaeus added that of Hermas as at least inspired, but not that of Peter. The Muratorian writer added that of Peter but not that of Hermas, but rejects Hermas in a way that suggests that Roman Christians had been wont to and indeed were still inclined to accept all three. Certainly more than one and probably three Christian apocalypses stood in the earliest New Testament at Rome about 185.

The first New Testament was thus a collection of collections. The chief groups of books which entered into it had been made long before, for other uses. The minor collections of apostolic letters and of revelations were made especially for it, though the books entering into them had long been written and had more or less currency as individual units among the churches. The Acts alone stands out as a solitary unit in the new collection, but its function as binding the various collections together is obvious.

The purpose of the new collection was to be read in church as scripture side by side with the Law and the Prophets and to serve as authoritative documents of apostolic origin in deciding what constituted genuine Christianity. It was an attempt to regulate and unify the written authorities that were read in church and appealed to in controversy, by limiting them to a fixed list.

Only books of apostolic origin were to be accepted in the new scripture. Hermas held his place for a while, as in Irenaeus, but only to be stricken from the list by the rigorous hand of the Muratorian writer. The apostles were now felt to be inspired in a higher sense than such erratic prophets as Montanus or even Hermas.

It is perhaps significant that this list as it appears in Irenaeus includes twenty-two books, just as Josephus' counting made the Jewish scriptures do. With Irenaeus, Christians began to call these books "scriptures," just as they did the Jewish books. Irenaeus does not actually call the new collection the New Testament. The first man who is known to have done that is probably an unknown writer of 192 A.D. who says in writing against the Montanists that he has not ventured to write against them earlier because of his dread of seeming to make some addition "to the Word (Logos) of the New Testament of the gospel which it is impossible for one who has chosen to live according to the gospel either to increase or to diminish."[6]

The first act in the drama of the formation of the New Testament ends with what the dramatists would call a full stage. The Acts, which had really introduced the drama by causing the collecting of Paul's letters, and had thereafter fallen into disuse if not neglect, once more appears to play an even more important part in binding together the two great groups in the final tableau. The Pauline collection appears enriched by the useful if unambitious pastoral letters. The great quartet of gospels culminating in John which had led to their first collection holds the center of the stage. A group of Christian apocalypses ascribed to apostolic authors and two or three letters named not for their readers like Paul's but for their supposedly apostolic writers help to fill out the heroic figures of the ancient apostles and give added color to the apostolic claims of the new scripture.

IX

THE NEW TESTAMENT AT
ALEXANDRIA

CHRISTIAN education began in Alexandria. About the middle of the second century there existed there a school for the instruction of Christian converts from paganism. To it there came probably about 180 a young man named Clement who threw himself into its work with such vigor that he became the assistant and at length the successor of its head, Pantaenus. He not only greatly influenced Christian thought all over the Eastern world through such pupils as Origen and Alexander of Jerusalem, but through the books he wrote between 190 and 212 he made a far wider and more lasting impression upon Christianity.

The first century of Christianity in Egypt is wrapped in obscurity. But by 150 two local gospels existed there, that of the Hebrews, which was current among Jewish Christians, and that of the Egyptians, which was in use among the Greek-speaking native population. The Logia, or Sayings of Jesus, found at Oxyrhynchus are probably collections of sayings selected from one or the other of these gospels, and made about the year 200 in Upper Egypt.[1] These gospels were in use in Egypt when the collected four gospels found their way there and began to compete with them. The local gospels were at first on a par with their new rivals, but soon fell into the background at Alexandria, before the greater wealth and variety and higher claims of the four. But the local gospels, although already overshadowed, had at the end of the century not yet come to be considered heretical. It is this stage of the development at Alexandria that is so clearly revealed in the works of Clement.

For the years that witnessed the conception and definition of the New Testament canon in the west saw also the first great literary expression of Alexandrian Christianity. The founder of that movement was Clement, and his mature life coincided in general with that of Tertullian. His extended writings give us our first clear picture of the Christianity of Alexandria, as it appeared to the most widely read Christian of his day. Had Alexandria a New Testament? What books belonged to it and how did they come to be there?

Clement did not hesitate to call himself a Christian Gnostic. He believed that the best values of Greek thought were not incompatible with Christian tradition, and he called one of his principal works Scrap-Books of Gnostic Notes on True Philosophy. He saw in Christianity the true philosophy, in which both Hebrew prophecy and Greek philosophy reached their culmination. Clement was very well read, especially in Christian literature. One of his principal works was his Outlines, which contained accounts of the books of scripture. If this work were still extant it would solve most of our doubts as to Clement's idea of the New Testament, but only portions of it have come down to us, in the works of Eusebius and Cassiodorus. In his Outlines, Eusebius says,[2] he gave concise accounts of the whole scriptures, "not passing over the disputed books: —I mean Jude and the Catholic epistles and Barnabas, and what is called the Revelation of Peter." But even without this important work, Clement's Address to the Greeks and his Tutor together with the Scrap-Books give us a fairly clear view of his Christian scripture.

With his wide literary sympathies, for he found the utterances of the Sibyl in accordance with revelation,[3] Clement accepted a larger group of Christian scriptures than his Roman contemporaries would have approved. In the first place, he quotes the gospels and some of the epistles of Paul as scripture just as he does the Old Testament, though less frequently. He credits such books with authority as expressing the mind and will of God. There is a fine liberality of view about Clement. He regards all good books as in a measure inspired, but the writings of the apostles are peculiarly so, because they possess a greater measure of truth, and so a higher authority, than other books.

Clement knew many gospels, but he gave the highest place among them to the four which he says "have been handed down to us." He knows also the Gospel of the Hebrews, the Gospel of the Egyptians, and the Traditions of Matthias, but while he does not regard them as heretical, he does not accept them as scripture. Indeed, the four gospels sometimes seem to stand in Clement upon a higher ground than any other Christian writings, even than those of Paul, probably because they contain so many sayings of Jesus.

Paul is usually referred to in Clement simply as "the apostle." Clement is the first writer to include Hebrews among his letters. With this step the Pauline collection reaches its fullest development. It had begun a century before with a collection of nine or ten letters, which was supplemented by the time of the founding of the Catholic church by the addition of the pastoral letters, I and II Timothy and Titus, and now finally at Alexandria the assignment of Hebrews to Paul completed the collection, increasing it to fourteen letters. Western writers had known Hebrews for a century, but had not connected it with the name of Paul nor considered it scripture. This step was taken by Clement at Alexandria, probably under the influence of his teacher Pantaenus, who had preceded him as head of the famous school there.[4] Clement often quotes "the noble apostle" with the same confidence that he feels for the Jewish scriptures.

The two great historic bodies of Christian literature were thus fully accepted at Alexandria in the last years of the second century. Beside them stood also as in the west a little group of Catholic or general letters—I Peter, I and II John, and Jude, the same letters which we have already found accepted in the west, although no single writer there up to this time shows acquaintance with all four. Clement quotes them somewhat more casually than he does the gospels or the letters of Paul. He introduces quotations from them briefly with the words "Peter says," "Jude says," "John says in the letter." Clement included them among the books which he summarized in his Outlines.

Clement also quotes the Letter of Clement of Rome to the Corinthians and the Letter of Barnabas as works of apostolic authority. This will seem less strange when it is remembered that the former stands after the Revelation in the Alexandrian Manuscript,[5] of the fifth century, and the latter in the same position in the Sinaitic Manuscript, of the fourth.[6] These are our most ancient complete Greek New Testaments. Clement was by no means alone in his reverence for these letters. We have seen that Eusebius speaks of the account he gives of Barnabas in his Outlines, where he evidently discussed it along with the Catholic, or general letters, as though he included it, with Jude, among them. Clement's collection of Catholic letters thus reached a total of six.

But it is in his attitude to Christian apocalypses, or revelations, that Clement is most interesting. He accepts the Revelation of John, the Revelation of Peter, and the Shepherd of Hermas. The last book especially had a marked influence upon him.[7] The objections which in the struggle with Montanism had already dislodged it from a place in Christian scripture in Rome and the west had not yet made themselves felt in Alexandria, where the earlier regard for the Shepherd still prevailed. Clement has the full collection of three apocalypses, John, Peter, and Hermas, which a few years earlier had been accepted at Rome, before the conflict with the prophets of Montanism had made the church suspicious of contemporary Christian prophecy. But in the east Hermas long continued to be considered scripture, and in the fourth-century Sinaitic Manuscript of the Bible it stands at the end of the New Testament. And the Revelation of Peter greatly expanded and under the title of Clement still stands after the Revelation of John in the Ethiopic New Testament.

We have seen that in each of the four main groups of the ancient New Testament Clement's scripture was remarkably full. He accepted all the gospels and revelations that the west had in its canon, and he had more Pauline and more Catholic letters than it. This fuller canon of scripture was characteristic of Alexandrian Christianity, and while not all that Clement accepted found a permanent place in the New

Testament, the influence of the Christian thinkers of Alexandria resulted in substantially enlarging the primitive Roman New Testament.

We have seen that the Acts of the Apostles
served an important structural purpose in the
early Roman New Testament, in binding together gospel and apostle and establishing the
continuity of Greek Christianity with the work
of Jesus and the twelve apostles. What was its
place in Clement? He knew it and quoted it as
the Acts of the Apostles and the work of Luke.
But did he consider it scripture? Did he indeed
draw a definite line among his Christian books
between those which were scripture and those
which were not? This question is acutely raised
by his use of Acts. He quotes it very much as
he does the Catholic letters, with no especial
mark of reverence but with familiarity and confidence, as though it were as well known to his
readers as to himself.

In much the same way Clement uses the
famous old Christian apology which went by
the name of the Preaching of Peter. He quotes
it with such expressions as "Peter says, in the
Preaching." Indeed, our knowledge of this lost
work is principally derived from Clement's quotations from it. Clement once quotes as scrip-

ture a saying found in the Teaching of the Apostles: "Son, be not a liar, for lying leads to theft."[8] In the same way he quotes as scripture other works unknown to us. "Take away from you the heavy yoke, and take up the easy one, says the scripture." "Ask, says the scripture, and I will do; think and I will give." But the strangest of his quotations is this: "The scripture exhorts us: Be ye skilful money-changers."

On the whole, Clement's canon of Christian scripture was not well defined. Just as he found truth in Plato and the other philosophers, and revelation or the beginnings of it in the Sibyl, he found his scriptures not only in the Jewish Bible and the four gospels and Paul, but in a number of lesser works some of which are now lost and forgotten.[9] Clement had no such hard-and-fast list of New Testament books as the churches of Rome and the west had in his day. In him we see the New Testament not fully formed, even in principle, but in process of formation, under the stress of religious and polemic needs. It was not the work of church councils but the result of personal and social needs which were finding their way gradually, in the course of the conflict with the sects and the development of church life, to a New Testament scripture.

88

X

THE AGE OF ORIGEN

THE greatest of Clement's pupils was Origen. He lived in an age of persecution. It was the persecution under Severus, which began in 202, that drove the mature Christian teachers out of Alexandria and brought Origen, when a youth of eighteen, to the headship of the Christian school at Alexandria. And it was the tortures he endured fifty years later in the Decian persecution that led to his death at Tyre in 254. The half-century lying between these dates was filled by Origen with a career of teaching, preaching, writing, and travel which made him the greatest thinker of his day and sent his influence far down the Christian centuries. His great learning and extraordinary talents were furthered by the help of his rich friend Ambrose, who, says Eusebius, provided him with seven amanuenses who relieved one another at appointed times.[1] "And he employed no fewer copyists, besides girls who were skilled in elegant writing." With such a staff it is no wonder that Origen stands out as the most prolific Christian writer of antiquity.

The confusion that prevailed in Clement's day as to what might be considered Christian scripture was not lost upon Origen. Unable to settle the problem for the churches, he took the one step the scholar can take; he analyzed it. He classified Christian scriptures as "acknowledged" or "disputed" and thus considerably simplified the situation. Clement and Origen probably stood between the unsophisticated Christian public at Alexandria, which was inclined to regard everything edifying as inspired, and the more circumspect western churches which, after their painful experience with Montanism and its prophetic claims, were disposed to limit inspiration to the apostles. In Clement the native Alexandrian breadth and enthusiasm predominated; in Origen the western circumspection was beginning to prevail, perhaps partly because he visited Rome and knew his great Roman contemporary Hippolytus.

Origen talked freely of the New Testament, as a collection of scripture of equal authority with the Old. "The canonical books," he says, "as the Hebrews have handed them down, are twenty-two, corresponding with the number of their letters."[2] His list of "acknowledged" New Testament books, that is, those accepted by all the churches as scripture, also amounts to twenty-two. He recognizes four gospels as the "only indisputable ones in the church of God." He knows many others, but dismisses them as heretical, thus going a step further than Clement had in his attitude to them. "The church," says Origen, "has four gospels, but the sects very many, one of which is entitled that According to the Egyptians, another that According to the Twelve Apostles."[3] The line between the four gospels and other gospels was thus much more sharply drawn by Origen than it had been by Clement. Only the four had been inspired.

Like Clement, Origen accepted fourteen letters of Paul. He is more conscious than Clement had been of the difficulty of thinking Paul to have been the author of Hebrews, but he continues to ascribe it to him, and thus helps to fix the Pauline collection at fourteen letters. Origen not only accepted Hebrews himself, but understood it to be generally accepted by the churches, that is, he placed it among the "acknowledged" books, although we know that it was not yet actually acknowledged in the west.[4]

The Acts of the Apostles also has a place in Origen's list of "acknowledged" books. So far his list is a very full one. But he recognized only two Catholic letters, I Peter and I John, as "acknowledged," and only one revelation—that of John. This made his list of "acknowledged" books up to twenty-two.

But this was not Origen's New Testament. He himself accepted several other books which he had the candor to recognize were not accepted by everybody. These he calls the "disputed" books. Foremost among these is the Letter of James, which Origen is the first Christian writer to treat as a part of the New Testament. Clement's collection of general letters consisted of I Peter, I and II John, Jude, Barnabas, and I Clement; Origen omits I Clement, and adds James, III John, and II Peter—which last, like James, makes its first appearance as a part of the New Testament in this "disputed" section of Origen's canon.

In the matter of apocalypses, Origen like Clement accepted the Shepherd of Hermas. Origen knew a great many other Christian books, but these twenty-nine—four gospels, fourteen letters of Paul, the Acts, eight Catholic letters, and two apocalypses—made up his own New Testament. The seven books in it which were not in his "acknowledged" list made up his "disputed" list. That is, Origen's "disputed" list contains the books which he accepts but some others reject.

In 1859 Tischendorf discovered at the Convent of St. Catharine on Mount Sinai a Greek manuscript of the Bible written probably in Egypt about a century after the death of Origen. In it the Revelation of John is followed by Barnabas and the Shepherd of Hermas. Its contents are thus just those of Origen's New Testament, and a note appended to one of its Old Testament books states that its text has been compared with a manuscript in the famous library at Caesarea which had been established there in the later years of the third century by his great admirer Pamphilus. It is a striking fact that our oldest complete New Testament contains the full list of twenty-nine New Testament books upon which the learned mind of Origen had settled in the early years of the third century. It was the hand of Origen which thus actually molded the New Testament canon of the Sinaitic Manuscript.[5]

When Origen as a young man still in the twenties visited Rome, he listened to the preaching of Hippolytus. Precocious as Origen was he was still a youth beside the great Hippolytus, then at the height of his powers, and the picture of the great genius of eastern Christianity sitting under the preaching of his greatest western contemporary is one to stir the imagination. They must have met and had some conversation, and certainly this Roman visit cannot have been without influence upon the active mind of Origen.

In character Hippolytus was a puritan, maintaining those ideals of Christian morality which Tertullian before him and Novatian later stood for. He wrote on many aspects of theology, but his Refutation of All Heresies is the work by which he is best known. A series of archaeological discoveries has helped to reveal the great shadowy figure of Hippolytus to the modern world. In 1551 there was discovered near the probable site of his grave outside of Rome the lower part of a statue of him, seated, and dressed as a philosopher. While the upper part of the figure was wanting, on the back of the chair was carved a list of the principal works of Hippolytus, which importantly supplemented the accounts of them given by ancient writers. Of his Refutation only the first book was extant, when in 1842 a manuscript containing practically all the rest of it was found on Mount Athos. Hippolytus had a long and serious controversy

94

with Callixtus, bishop of Rome, over matters of church discipline. In 235, during the persecution of Maximin, he was banished to Sardinia, and shortly after he died. He was the last Roman Christian to write his works in Greek, but many of his works have disappeared in Greek and are extant only in fragments in ancient oriental translations. His literary remains are now considerable enough, however, to enable us to form a clear picture of his New Testament.

Hippolytus was a pupil of Irenaeus, and it is not strange that his New Testament closely resembles that of his teacher. Hippolytus regarded the four gospels · as scripture. He accepted the thirteen letters of Paul, not including Hebrews. We have seen that this was the Roman view of the Pauline collection; and Hippolytus' famous contemporary Gaius of Rome held the same view of the Pauline canon. Hippolytus accepted Acts and three Catholic letters—I Peter, and I and II John. The Revelation of John was the only apocalypse in his New Testament. This makes a New Testament of twenty-two books.

Hippolytus was acquainted with many other books which before or after his time found a place in the New Testament. He knew the

Letter to the Hebrews, the Shepherd of Hermas, the Revelation of Peter, the Acts of Paul, and many more. In his writings for the first time we find II Peter reflected, which Origen a little later included in his New Testament. Hippolytus once quotes the first verse of James with the words, "As the saying of Jude in his first letter to the Twelve Tribes proves."[6] This suggests acquaintance with both James and Jude, but not very intimate acquaintance.

After Hippolytus, Roman Christians wrote in Latin, and the bond of a common language which had tended to hold eastern and western Christianity somewhat together was withdrawn. East and west differed materially as to what books belonged to the New Testament, and the approach to unity with regard to it was probably further deferred by the rise of the barrier of language. A few years after the death of Hippolytus, and about the time of the death of Origen, we find Novatian of Rome and Cyprian of Carthage engaged in a correspondence, in Latin, on church matters. In these letters and in their treatises they show very much the same canon as that used by Hippolytus. Cyprian's quotations are especially full and show that his New Testament was precisely that of Hippolytus, except for II John. But that is quoted by another North African writer of his day, and so clearly belonged to the New Testament there.

Thus in the middle of the third century while eastern Christianity under the influence of Origen was expanding the New Testament earlier sketched by Rome, the western churches still cherished its more primitive form. The initial collections of gospels and of Pauline letters had been formed long before in Asia, probably at Ephesus. At Rome these had been united and expanded into the first New Testament. At Alexandria this was further supplemented by the inclusion of six or seven books which greatly appealed to the eastern mind. The pendulum had reached one extreme at Rome, and another at Alexandria, and it was long to continue to swing before it came to rest.

XI

FROM ORIGEN TO EUSEBIUS

WHEN in 230 the hostility of Demetrius the bishop drove Origen to leave Alexandria and establish a school at Caesarea, his pupil and assistant Heraclas became the head of the school at Alexandria. In the following year Heraclas became bishop of Alexandria, and Dionysius succeeded him as the head of the school which Clement and Origen had made so famous. Sixteen years later, at the death of Heraclas, Dionysius once more succeeded him, this time as bishop of Alexandria. His long episcopate of seventeen years (247–64) was one succession of persecutions and other disasters—pestilence, famine, and civil wars. More than once imprisoned or banished, Dionysius nevertheless so energetically and ably met the situation with letters and treatises that he became a world-figure. Eusebius refers to him as "Dionysius, the great bishop of Alexandria,"[1] and he lives in history as Dionysius the Great.

In his work On Promises Dionysius discusses the Revelation of John with extraordinary keenness.[2] He respects the work very greatly, though he admits he does not understand it, but he cannot accept the view that it is by the author of the Gospel and Letters of John. Everything about it leads him to think its author was some other John, and not the apostle of that name. That the bishop of Alexandria could thus express himself about the greatest of Christian apocalypses in the third quarter of the third century shows how uncertain was the status of the Revelation in the churches of the east, and helps us to understand the next great figure in the history of the New Testament, Eusebius of Caesarea, the Father of Church History.

At Caesarea a devoted admirer of Origen named Pamphilus had established a school and assembled a library which in its collection of Christian works, especially Origen's, and of manuscripts of the Greek Bible surpassed all others.[3] To this school came the young Eusebius, and there acquired the great learning which afterward distinguished him. He became greatly attached to his teacher Pamphilus, and in his honor he liked to call himself "Eusebius the son of Pamphilus."

Eusebius became the bishop of Caesarea and the friend and biographer of Constantine, with whom he participated in the great Council of Nicaea, in 325. His greatest work is his Church History, which brings its narrative down to about 325 A.D. It is a history not only of the church but of its literature. Eusebius had made good use of the library of Pamphilus, and when he mentions a book he usually takes the pains to review it and even to quote some characteristic passages from it. Not a few works of the second and third centuries are actually best known to us today by the fragments of them thus preserved by Eusebius.

This marked literary interest makes what Eusebius has to say about the New Testament of especial importance. Eusebius like Origen recognized the disagreement that prevailed as to the precise contents of the New Testament, and like Origen he attempted no more than to analyze the problem. Apart from the works of the schismatics, he recognized certain books as "acknowledged" and certain others as "disputed."[4] Some of the "disputed" books he, and probably the prevalent opinion in the east, considered canonical, and accepted as part of the New Testament. Others of them which were going out of favor with the churches he designated as "rejected," by which he probably meant no more than "uncanonical." His own New Testament is therefore to be found in the combination of his "acknowledged" list with those "disputed" books which he does not dismiss as "rejected." It would have been clearer if he had used some special term to distinguish these preferred books, but he failed to do so, and thus left his account of the canon of the New Testament somewhat confused.

Eusebius' New Testament begins with what he calls the "holy quaternion of gospels." This was followed by the Acts of the Apostles and this by the letters of Paul. Then came I John and I Peter and after them, "if it really seem proper," cautiously remarks Eusebius, the Revelation of John. These were the accepted or acknowledged books. As Eusebius included Hebrews among the letters of Paul, making the list of his letters fourteen, his acknowledged books numbered twenty-two, and they were just the twenty-two regarded as "acknowledged" by Origen. Only in his uncertainty about the status of the Revelation of John does Eusebius differ, but that is not serious enough to lead him to omit it from the "acknowledged" class.

As disputed books which are yet not uncanonical Eusebius classes James, Jude, II Peter, and II and III John. This group, combined with the "acknowledged" books, made up his New Testament, which like ours contained twenty-seven books.

The disputed books listed by Eusebius as rejected were the Acts of Paul, the Shepherd, the Revelation of Peter, the Letter of Barnabas, the Teaching of the Apostles, "and besides, as I said, the Revelation of John, if it seem proper, which some, as I said, reject, but which some class with the accepted books."[5] It is clear that the Revelation of John has lost ground in the east since Origen's time, as we should expect from the criticism offered by Dionysius the Great of its supposed apostolic authorship. Eusebius goes on to say that some have placed the Gospel according to the Hebrews among the "rejected" writings.

Over against these ecclesiastical books, Eusebius puts the heretical works which have no claim of any kind to a place in the canon of scripture. Such are the gospels of Peter, of Thomas, and of Matthias, and the Acts of Andrew and of John. In giving his reasons for repudiating these works Eusebius reveals his test of canonicity. To belong to the New Testament a book must be of apostolic origin, and that may be determined by its use by earlier ecclesiastical writers and its freedom from heretical ideas.

In Eusebius we observe a somewhat stricter drawing of the line among the disputed books between those that were canonical and those that were not. Origen had recognized Barnabas and the Shepherd as canonical. Eusebius does not. On the other hand, the Revelation of John is no longer in any real sense undisputed, although Eusebius cannot realize it. Its place in the canon is beginning to be insecure.

Eusebius' canon had very practical fruits in his own day, for the Christian emperor Constantine commissioned him to provide fifty copies of the scriptures for the churches of his new capital Constantinople, and we may suppose that Eusebius saw to it that they contained the twenty-seven New Testament books that he believed to be canonical.

There is in Paris a manuscript of the letters of Paul in Greek and Latin, written in the sixth century and called from its former home the Clermont Manuscript.[6] Just before the Letter to the Hebrews the scribe copied into the manuscript a list in Latin of the books of the Old and New Testaments. The peculiar contents of the

New Testament list show that it must be of Egyptian origin, and must go back to a list made there about the year 300. It probably represents a more popular if less intelligent view of the canon than that of the learned and traveled Eusebius, and well illustrates the powerful bent toward a full canon that characterized the early Christianity of Egypt.

The New Testament list begins with the four gospels and the letters of Paul. Four of these seem to have been omitted from the list through the carelessness of the scribe, for the particular ten that he gives have as a list no parallel in the history of the canon. Eight Catholic letters follow—those of Peter, James, John, Jude, and Barnabas. The list concludes with three revelations and two books of acts curiously arranged to alternate—the Revelation of John, the Acts of the Apostles, the Shepherd of Hermas, the Acts of Paul, the Revelation of Peter. The scribe, or some later hand, put a dash before I Peter, Barnabas, Hermas, the Acts of Paul, and the Revelation of Peter; before I Peter probably to indicate that with it the Catholic letters begin; with the rest perhaps to indicate doubt of their right in such a list; they may have been so marked in the original list made in Egypt in Greek about the year 300. If so, the list presents a very close parallel to what we have seen in Origen and Eusebius, both of whom recognize a group of books on the very borders of the canon, sometimes included in it and sometimes shut out. The list of these doubtful books is very much the same in Eusebius and the Clermont list; only the Teaching of the Apostles and the Gospel according to the Hebrews which Eusebius calls disputed are absent from the Clermont list. The important fact is that in the Clermont list the distinction between the "acknowledged" books and the "disputed" canonical ones has disappeared. Only the line separating the rejected books from all the rest remains.

Thus the exact boundaries of the New Testament continued to fluctuate in Egypt and Palestine in the third and early fourth centuries, and of the earlier fringe of doubtful books some are more and more accepted and some more and more rejected, while in the midst of the ebb and flow we catch the first glimpse of the New Testament as we know it, in the form of it which Eusebius personally approved.

XII

ATHANASIUS AND OUR NEW TESTAMENT

AT THE Council of Nicaea in 325 Alexander, bishop of Alexandria, was attended by a young man named Athanasius, who was his arch-deacon. Five months later, Alexander died, and Athanasius, at the age of thirty-three, became his successor. Athanasius' episcopate of nearly fifty years was broken by intervals of banish-ment and expulsion, but in that long period with its heated controversies he came to stand as the leading champion of the positions taken at Ni-caea. His travels took him now to Constanti-nople, now to Rome; he was banished to Gaul, visited Belgium, or took refuge in Upper Egypt; in one way or another he saw the world, and he saw it as one of its leading figures.

It was the custom of many bishops to ad-dress a letter at Easter to the churches in their dioceses, and Athanasius wrote one such Easter letter that has great importance for the New Testament canon. It was in 367, a year after his return from the last of his exiles, that he wrote his famous letter on the books of scripture.[1] He was now over seventy years old, and knew the Christian world of his day, east and west, as few men did.

Athanasius' New Testament begins with the four gospels—According to Matthew, According to Mark, According to Luke, and According to John. "Then after these are the Acts of the Apostles and the Letters of the Apostles called Catholic, seven of them:—of James, one, of Peter, two, of John, three, and after these one of Jude. In addition there are fourteen letters of Paul the apostle." Athanasius gives these in the following order: Romans, Corinthians (two), Galatians, Ephesians, Philippians, Colossians, Thessalonians (two), Hebrews, Timothy (two), Titus, Philemon. His list ends with the Revelation of John.

These alone are the New Testament scriptures, but Athanasius adds to them as a kind of supplement a few books produced, he says, "by our ancestors to be read by those who are just coming forward to receive oral instruction in religion." Five of these books for catechumens are from what we know as the Old Testament Apocrypha. The other two are the Teaching of the Apostles and the Shepherd of Hermas. In his earlier writings Athanasius had made frequent use of the Shepherd, once apparently treating it as scripture, as so many had done before him. But his final position is that while it is useful for Christian instruction, it has no place in the New Testament.

Athanasius goes on to decry the "secret" books (apocrypha) appealed to by the sects, and to warn believers against them. It was the currency of these, and the practice of some to "arrange for themselves the so-called secret writings and to mingle them with the inspired scriptures," he says, that has moved him to make this the subject of his letter. The list of Athanasius is therefore a part of the long fight against the schismatics and a further illustration of the part that conflict had in the process of fixing a New Testament scripture. The Old and New Testament books, Athanasius concludes, are the divine writings, the inspired scripture, the springs of salvation. "In them alone is the good news of the teaching of true religion proclaimed: let no one add to them or take away aught of them." Athanasius did not write his list because everybody was now agreed upon it, but on the contrary because, among the heretics at least, other views existed. At the same time his list was not original with him, but probably reflected the best Catholic, that is, non-schismatic, practice of his time, as he, with his wide acquaintance with Christian usage all over the world of his day, had come to see it.

Athanasius' New Testament was evidently just like our own, containing twenty-seven books. Eusebius' misgivings about the Revelation of John were not shared by Athanasius, whose faith in that book may have been strengthened by the years he spent in the west, where the Revelation was generally accepted. The most striking exception to this western acceptance of the Revelation is in the Gothic New Testament of Ulfilas, a younger contemporary of Athanasius, famous as the apostle to the Goths and the translator of the New Testament into Gothic. The Revelation was not included in Ulfilas' version, but his Arian theology separated him from Athanasius, who would hardly have been influenced by what Ulfilas thought of the Revelation even if he knew of it.

In the two books which Athanasius recommends for the use of young people and new converts we recognize writings which had long been dear to the average Christian of Egypt, and had been on the fringes of the New Testament of

Eusebius and the Clermont Manuscript. In Athanasius, as in the Clermont list, Origen's old division between "acknowledged" and "disputed" has disappeared, and in that list we have in fact a kind of middle term between Eusebius and Athanasius.

The Egyptian background of Athanasius' canon is somewhat illumined by what we know of the Coptic Christianity of his day. Native Egyptian Christianity arose through contact with the Greek Christianity of Alexandria and of Upper Egypt. Between 250 and 350 the Sahidic, the earliest Coptic version of the New Testament or parts of it, began to take shape. The first books to be put into that dialect so far as we can judge included the Revelation of John; indeed all the books of Athanasius' New Testament were in the Sahidic New Testament. We should expect this harmony, for Athanasius spent some time among the monks of Upper Egypt, and St. Anthony and Pachomius, the founders of Egyptian monasticism, were his friends. The Shepherd of Hermas also passed into a Sahidic version, and this in turn led to an Ethiopic version of it which still exists. A Sahidic manuscript of I Clement has been found dating from the second half of the fourth century—the very time of Athanasius. The Acts of Paul are now chiefly known to us from an Akhmimic-Sahidic version. The existence of these texts in Sahidic show that when Sahidic literature arose, these books were in high favor with native Egyptian Christianity, and passed into Sahidic side by side with the books recognized by Alexandrian authorities as scripture. The Sahidic canon was probably less rigidly fixed and still had more of the old Egyptian inclusiveness and breadth than the Greek canon of the time.

The three oldest Greek manuscripts of the New Testament that are most nearly complete come from Egypt, and two of these were written in the lifetime of Athanasius. We may naturally look to them for additional light on the New Testament canon of Greek Christianity in Egypt in his age and the one that followed. The oldest of the three unfortunately breaks off abruptly at Heb. 9:14; the remaining leaves are lost. They doubtless contained the remaining books of our New Testament, but was that all? Did the Vatican manuscript originally end with the Revelation? We cannot say, but judging by the contents of the other two it probably did not. The Sinaitic manuscript, written in the second half of the fourth century, has Barnabas and the opening part of the Shepherd of Hermas after the Revelation,[2] thus reflecting the canon of Origen; and the Alexandrian manuscript written early in the fifth century and probably in Alexandria has I and II Clement after the Revelation.[3] The voice of Athanasius did not therefore settle the matter of what belonged to the New Testament, even for Greek Christianity in Egypt.

It is a striking fact that the early councils had so little to say about determining the books of scripture. They were greatly concerned with theological definition, but the New Testament canon was left to develop informally among the churches, now and again being molded by the hand of some masterful personality like Athanasius or the Roman author of the Muratorian canon. It was not until near the close of the fourth century that more formal and official measures were taken with regard to it by the decrees of councils. But in the period that followed it was in no small degree the influence of the great Athanasius that carried the day for his canon of the New Testament and thus eventually made it also ours.

Since Athanasius' New Testament was like our own, it might seem that with his Easter letter of 367 the story of the New Testament canon was ended. But in another part of the east very different views of the proper contents of the New Testament still prevailed, and the story of the New Testament canon now takes us from Egypt to Syria.

XIII

THE NEW TESTAMENT IN SYRIA

CHRISTIANITY, it has been truly said, remained a Greek movement almost to the end of the second century. Its success among the Jews was small. It very early passed over into the Greek world and it was the Greeks' ready acceptance of it that carried it over the Roman Empire and opened to it the door of the future.

Through much of the first and nearly all of the second century it was through Greek channels and among people of Greek culture that Christianity spread. Thus it happened that the New Testament books were written in Greek. Even at Rome the church was Greek in language down to the days of Hippolytus, who died in 236.

It was the missionary zeal of Paul and men like him that had made Christianity a Greek movement and carried the gospel to the west, and it was missionary zeal that a century and a quarter later carried it back again from Rome to Syria. Legend traces the beginnings of Syriac Christianity to the very days of Jesus himself, but the probability is that it owed its principal impulse to the work of Tatian the Syrian—the pupil of Justin at Rome and afterward the apostle to Syria.

It was about 170 that Tatian returned to the east, and having combined the four gospels into one continuous Syriac narrative under the name of the Diatessaron, a Greek expression equivalent to our word "four-ply," entered that hinterland of Syriac-speaking Syria of which Edessa was the capital. That he should have combined the four gospels in this way shows how free he was from any canonical reverence for them, but that he should have used this interweaving of them to the exclusion of the separate gospels themselves in his very effective missionary work shows it more clearly still. Whatever Tatian may have thought of Paul's letters—and his Address to the Greeks shows acquaintance with several of them—he did not consider them scripture, nor introduce them into Syria along with his Diatessaron. Eusebius says that he even undertook to re-write them in an improved style.[1] In short, it is clear that when Tatian left Rome on his mission, soon after 170, the conception of a New Testament as a collection of scripture had not arisen there. Tatian's mission was a pronounced success, and his Diatessaron became and long remained the recognized gospel of interior Syria. It has come to light in modern times in an Arabic version, which was published in 1888 at Rome, but no copy of the Syriac original has yet been found.

When in the closing years of the second century the Catholic movement made itself felt at Antioch, efforts were made to relate this Syriac Christianity with the Greek Christianity of Antioch, and Serapion, bishop of Antioch (193–209), about 200 consecrated Palut bishop of Edessa. It was this Serapion who suppressed the Gospel of Peter in the parish of Rhossos near Antioch upon learning its Docetic character, that is, its representation of Christ's sufferings as unreal.[2] This aversion for apocryphal gospels would naturally be felt by a Catholic bishop of Antioch, and a similar feeling probably led Palut at Edessa to seek to introduce the New Testament scriptures there. To such an effort we probably owe the two manuscripts of the four separate gospels in Syriac that have come to light in the past century, bearing the name Evangelion da Mepharreshe[3]—"the Gospel of the Separates"—to distinguish them from the Evangelion da Mehallete—"the Gospel of the

Mixed"—that is, the Diatessaron. These manuscripts were actually written in the fourth or
fifth centuries, but they evidently go back to a
text as old as the beginning of the third. It is
probable that this ancient gospel text reflects
an early effort made under Catholic influence by
Palut or his successors to replace the Diatessaron, which was unknown to Greek Catholic
Christianity, by the fourfold gospel which was
the cornerstone of the New Testament. But it
did not shake the position of the Diatessaron
which was already established in Syria through
the work of Tatian and his followers as the
gospel.

It must be remembered that the Syriac
church was founded by Tatian, who was not
considered orthodox, and it was at first strongly
influenced by the Christian poet Bardaisan
(154–222), who was more or less tinged with
Gnosticism. It was not therefore in line with the
Catholic movement of the Greek world, from
which it was far removed in language, place, and
culture.

Our next glimpse of the progress of the New
Testament in Syria comes from the quaint document called the Teaching of Addai, which was
written toward the middle of the fourth cen-

tury.[4] It describes the Christians of Syria as hearing the "New Testament of the Diatessaron" read along with the Old Testament.

"The Law and the Prophets and the Gospel, in which you read every day before the people, and the Letters of Paul which Simon Cephas sent us from the city of Rome, and the Acts of the Twelve Apostles which John the son of Zebedee sent us from Ephesus,—in these writings shall you read in the churches of Christ, and along with them you shall read nothing else besides, for there is nothing else wherein is written the truth that you possess beside these writings."

The New Testament of Syria at this time evidently consisted of the Diatessaron, the letters of Paul, and the Acts of the Apostles, but the Acts and the letters were recognized as additions made to the primitive Syriac scripture under the Catholic influence of Rome and Ephesus. And only the "Gospel," that is, the Diatessaron, is in daily church use side by side with the Old Testament. The gradual growth of the Syriac scripture from the Diatessaron as a beginning is clearly reflected in this legend. To Peter and John, great apostolic figures of Catholic tradition, Syrian piety in the fourth century

ascribed these Catholic additions to its scripture, which had come to it, just as Catholic
thought conceived them, as a heritage from the
apostles. But these did not yet equal the Diatessaron, the oldest part of the Syrian scripture.
And as for the Catholic letters or the apocalypses
so important in other canons of the time, they
were as yet quite unknown to Syriac scripture.

The sermons of the Syriac-speaking Persian
Afrahat written toward the middle of the fourth
century confirm the testimony of the Teaching
of Addai. Afrahat knew the Diatessaron, the letters of Paul—including Hebrews, the Pastorals,
and perhaps even the apocryphal III Corinthians—and the Acts. He was also acquainted
with the Gospel of John and perhaps the other
separate gospels. Efrem, the great Syriac father
of the fourth century, who died in 373, wrote a
commentary on the Diatessaron and on the full
list of Paul's letters, including III Corinthians,
which passed from the Syriac into the ancient
Armenian New Testament. The Acts completed
Efrem's New Testament canon. He also knew
the four separate gospels, but it was not they but
the Diatessaron that was scripture for Efrem.
Efrem traveled about the world and knew the
Revelation and some of the Catholic letters—

I Peter, I John, and perhaps James—but not as parts of the New Testament.

It is plain that in the fourth century the fourfold gospel (Matthew, Mark, Luke, and John) was once more coming forward to challenge the primacy of the Diatessaron. A further stage in this process is reflected in a Syriac canon of the Old and New Testaments of about 400, found in the Convent of St. Catharine on Mount Sinai.[5] It contains the four separate gospels, the Acts, and fourteen letters of Paul. "This is all," adds the writer of the list. His New Testament is like that of the Teaching of Addai, of Afrahat and of Efrem, only now the separate gospels have replaced the Diatessaron, and its long and extraordinary reign of two centuries in Syria is over.

The great step in the history of the Syriac New Testament was taken in the time of Rabbula, who was bishop of Edessa from 411 to 435. Tradition declares that he ordered the separate gospels put in every church and read, and that he produced a version or revision of the New Testament in Syriac. This can only refer to the appearance of the Peshitto New Testament, the standard Syriac version, toward which events had now been tending for more than a century. This version is represented by a great many manuscripts, some of them as old as the fifth and sixth centuries. It contains the four gospels, the Acts, three Catholic letters—James, I Peter, and I John—and fourteen letters of Paul.[6] The primitive character of this canon, with its short list of Catholic letters, and the absence of the Revelation, is apparent, yet it is a fuller canon than Edessa had previously accepted. In fact, throughout its history North Syria seems to lag behind the other parts of the Christian world in the development of its New Testament scripture.

The Peshitto must have won a very swift and complete victory over ancient forms of the New Testament in Syria, for when the Jacobite controversy over the nature of Christ in 431 divided the church, both sects kept the Peshitto as their New Testament scripture. The Nestorian schism of 489 did not impair this dominion of the Peshitto, and in all their subsequent wanderings over both hemispheres the scattered children of the North Syrian church have clung to that version. Its differences from the canons of the peoples around them have only tended to fix it more firmly in the esteem of Syrians.

Not that the victory of the Peshitto was easily won. Theodoret, who became bishop of Cyrrhus west of the Euphrates about 423, records that he found more than two hundred copies of the Diatessaron held in honor among the churches, which he gathered together and replaced with the gospels of the four evangelists. This must have been done by other energetic churchmen all over North Syria, with such success that while Peshitto manuscripts are plentiful, no Syriac copy of the Diatessaron has yet been found.

The Peshitto was itself later revised, but these revisions had little real effect upon Syrian usage. The first was made in 508 by a rural bishop Polycarp for Philoxenus, bishop of Mabog in West Syria. While the East Syrians, being farthest from the Greek influence of Antioch, looked with disfavor upon the presence of Catholic letters in the New Testament, West Syrian churchmen like Philoxenus and Polycarp in revising the Peshitto on the basis of Greek manuscripts admitted all seven Catholic letters and even the Revelation of John to their revised New Testament.

A century later, in 616, this Philoxenian version was revised in its turn by Thomas of Harkel at Alexandria, with the aid of Greek manuscripts which he found there. In contents his revision follows the version of Philoxenus, who thus has the distinction of introducing the Revelation and the lesser Catholic letters into the canon of Syria. Dionysius bar Salibi, indeed, who died in 1171, wrote a commentary on the Revelation, and evidently regarded it as scripture, but the place of the Revelation and the lesser Catholic letters was often only nominal, since the Peshitto continued to be copied and read without them, and the Philoxenian and Harklensian versions found little favor compared with that everywhere enjoyed by it.

Even this does not complete the list of the Syriac versions. For in the sixth century, that is, between the date of the Philoxenian and the Harklensian, there was produced probably under the influence of Antioch a translation of the New Testament into the Palestinian dialect of Syriac, which prevailed in the vicinity of Antioch. Our knowledge of this version is chiefly gained from a number of lectionaries or church lesson-books, and these included not only the four gospels, the Acts, and the fourteen letters of Paul, but certainly I and II Peter and I John, and therefore presumably all seven of the Catholic letters. Only the Revelation remains doubtful, and from what we have seen of its neglect in the Syrian canons and what seems to have been its disuse in Antioch, it is very possible that it was wanting from the Palestinian Syriac version of the sixth century. The version was probably one result of the efforts made by Justinian to force Christianity upon the Jews and Samaritans of Palestine. It experienced a revival in the eleventh century, and about that time most of the extant manuscripts of it were written.

Thus in a little Syrian world of its own, and yet almost under the shadow of the Greek Christianity of Antioch, arose the Syriac New Testament. All along its course, from the conflict between the Diatessaron and the separate gospels, through the New Testaments of Addai, Afrahat, and Efrem to the Peshitto, the influence of Antioch can be traced. As the point of contact of Syrian Christianity with the Greek world, Antioch more or less steadily influenced Syria toward conformity with Catholic scripture and usage. But Syria, too, had its influence upon Antioch, sometimes in a striking personality like Lucian of Antioch (†312), who was educated at Edessa, but chiefly as a conservative background steadily opposed to the enlargement of scripture. As Egyptian Christianity with its liberal view of inspiration influenced Alexandria toward a larger New Testament, Syrian Christianity influenced Antioch toward a smaller one. And with Antioch we are introduced to Chrysostom and the age of the councils.

XIV

THE AGE OF THE COUNCILS

THE New Testament is sometimes spoken of as the work of councils. But as a matter of fact it was well defined in contents and position before the councils took it up, and when they did, it was only to indorse views about it that already prevailed. In 363 the Synod of Laodicea in Asia Minor, in its fifty-ninth canon, forbade the reading of uncanonical books. It assumed that it was well known what books were canonical, but in some copies of its canons a sixtieth is added, in which a list of biblical books is given. It is not, therefore, a part of the actual findings of that synod, although it is in all probability a fourth-century list. It includes all the books of our New Testament except the Revelation.

The Council of Hippo in Africa, however, in 393 laid down our present New Testament list as scripture. The Synod of Carthage in 397 declares that nothing should be read in church as divine scripture except the canonical scriptures. It proceeds to give the list of the Old and New

Testament books, the latter just as we have them, and adds that on the martyrs' days their martyrdoms may be read.[1] The contrast between east and west in the matter of the acceptance of the Revelation is clearly seen in these two lists. The west accepts the Revelation, the east rejects it. The canon of 397 was reaffirmed at the next council of Carthage, in 419, except that Hebrews, which had been listed separately from the other Pauline letters in 397, is included among them in 419. In these councils Augustine took a leading part, and in the matter of the New Testament his influence in them was probably decisive. Indeed, the development of the New Testament canon in this eventful period can only be understood by reviewing some of the great figures of the time and recalling how they stood on the debatable matters of Hebrews, the Catholic letters, and the Revelation.

Of all the interpreters of the New Testament John Chrysostom is the greatest. Born at Antioch about 347 he studied under Libanius and then under Diodorus of Tarsus, and became a presbyter in Antioch. The fame of his preaching led to his appointment in 398 as patriarch of Constantinople, and there his fearless denunciation of the evils of court, monks, and clergy brought about his banishment which ended in 407 in his death. He was the greatest of the Greek preachers, and the immense popularity of his works in the Greek world has preserved great numbers of his sermons, which have largely shaped the interpretation of the New Testament from that day to this.

So copiously is the New Testament quoted in the sermons of Chrysostom that one can almost reconstruct a full text of his New Testament from his quotations. His famous Synopsis of Holy Scripture names as the books of the New Testament fourteen letters of Paul, four gospels, the Acts, and three Catholic letters.[2] This is just the canon of the Peshitto, and reflects the usage of Antioch about the end of the fourth century. With this list, Chrysostom's own use of New Testament books in his sermons fully agrees. In them he makes no use of the four minor Catholic letters or the Revelation as scripture.

We have seen Ephesus forming the earliest collections of Christian books, and Rome shaping these into the first New Testament. We have seen Alexandria expanding this Roman New Testament into much ampler proportions. And now at the beginning of the fifth century

Antioch puts its hand to the shaping of the New Testament, guiding the Peshitto revision of the Syriac, the oldest of the versions, and through Chrysostom speaking in the capital of the Greek world for the same canon of twenty-two books, the canon of Antioch. The conservative voice of Antioch utters its strongest word on the contents of the New Testament at this time.

Great as was the influence of Chrysostom upon the understanding of the New Testament, in the matter of its canon his example did not prevail. His younger contemporary, Theodoret of Cyrrhus (386–458), shares with him the canon of Antioch, where both had grown up. But the other great Antiochian, Theodore, who became bishop of Mopsuestia, in Cilicia, about 392, and lived until 428, held other views. Like Chrysostom, Theodore was a native of Antioch, and a pupil of Libanius. His New Testament included neither the Revelation nor any Catholic letters, so that its contents were just those of that Syriac list of about 400 which we have already considered in connection with the New Testament in Syria. Theodore was a man of great learning and ability, and was in some ways the greatest figure of the school of Antioch, although as a preacher and interpreter he did not equal Chrysostom. In Theodore even more than in Chrysostom we see the tendency of Antioch toward a shorter New Testament.

Two eminent Christian leaders of Asia Minor in this period show the variety of opinion about the New Testament that existed toward the close of the fourth century. Gregory of Nazianzus in Cappadocia (329–89), a great preacher and theologian, is reckoned one of the four "doctors" of the eastern church, sharing this distinction with Athanasius, Chrysostom, and Basil. His New Testament list included the four gospels, the Acts, fourteen letters of Paul, and seven Catholic letters. "You have them all," concludes Gregory.[3] The notable thing here is the absence of the Revelation. This form of the New Testament is that of the sixtieth canon of Laodicea already mentioned, and also reappears in the later List of the Sixty Canonical Books. Amphilochius, of Iconium in Asia Minor, was a famous contemporary of Gregory's, and gives us another glimpse of the canon in his day. Amphilochius, who died in 394, admitted to the New Testament the four gospels, the Acts, and fourteen letters of Paul, noting that some call Hebrews uncanonical, but are wrong in doing so.[4] "Of Catholic letters," he goes on, "some say seven, others only three,—one of James, one of Peter, and one of John's." "The Revelation of John some accept but the majority call it uncanonical." This curious statement shows the breadth of Amphilochius' information. He knows that some churches, probably in the west, question Hebrews. And in fact the first western writer to accept Hebrews as entitled to a place in the New Testament was Hilary of Poitiers, who died in 367. In the east, however, Hebrews had been generally accepted from Clement of Alexandria on. Amphilochius is well aware of the two opinions as to the Catholic letters, and leaves us in some uncertainty as to whether he accepted three or seven. But he seems to agree with Chrysostom, Theodore, and Gregory in rejecting the Revelation.

On the other hand, Basil († 379), Gregory of Nyssa († about 394), and Epiphanius of Constantia in Cyprus († 403) like Athanasius accepted the Revelation. That book thus divided the east at the end of the fourth century. This comes out clearly in the fact that of the most venerated Greek fathers, the four doctors of the eastern church, two accepted the Revelation and two rejected it. Only gradually in the centuries that followed did it make its way into acceptance as a part of the canon of the Greek church, and to this day Greek Christianity has no readings from the Revelation in its church lessons.

In the west, on the other hand, the uncertainty attached not to the Revelation but to Hebrews. We have seen that in the middle of the third century, when Roman Christianity began to use Latin, it still omitted Hebrews from the letters of Paul and accepted only three Catholic letters—I Peter and I and II John. Thereafter the further development of the New Testament went on in the east, where we have traced its growth. What was the western attitude to this development?

About 359, a century after the time of Cyprian, an unknown North African writer made a list of the books of the Bible and the works of Cyprian. His New Testament list consisted of four gospels, thirteen letters of Paul, the Acts, the Apocalypse, three letters of John, and two of Peter. The resemblance of this to Cyprian's canon is very close; its only additions to Cyprian are II and III John and II Peter. And a reviser has even here restored Cyprian's list by adding after John and Peter the words "one only."[5]

In the half-century that followed, Latin

Christianity was rich in great names, and it is easy to trace the fortunes of the parts of the New Testament canon that were still in doubt. Hilary of Poitiers (†367) and the mysterious Ambrosiaster, perhaps a converted Jew, treat Hebrews as canonical, and Lucifer of Cagliari in Sardinia (†371) included it among the letters of Paul, having perhaps learned to do so in the years he spent in exile in the east. Priscillian of Saragossa, the Spanish martyr (†385), also accepted Hebrews as Paul's. Pelagius of Britain indeed did not include it in his Commentary on Paul's Letters which he wrote at Rome about 410, but the great figures of Ambrose, Rufinus, Jerome, and Augustine made its victory in the west secure. Jerome, the great reviser of the Latin Bible, included it in his famous Vulgate version undertaken in 382,[6] but repeatedly mentions the Latin suspicion of it: "The custom of the Latins does not accept it." "Among the Romans to this day it is not considered Paul's." Augustine at first considers it Paul's but later calls it anonymous. Yet he does not question its place in the canon, and acknowledges that the example of the eastern churches has influenced him to accept it.[7] He in turn influenced the North African Councils of Hippo (393) and

Carthage (397, 419) to include it in their New Testament lists. The last of these, held at Carthage in 419, is careful to make it clear that its canon is only a suggestion, offered to the Church at Rome for its official indorsement. Even this degree of uncertainty is surprising fifty years after Athanasius' festal letter of 367, until we remember that east and west were going their own ways, and even in the east it was the influence rather than the authority of Athanasius that led to the general acceptance of his list.

The eastern list of seven Catholic letters came even more slowly into general acceptance in the west. Hilary, Lucifer, and Ambrose accepted three or four Catholics; Priscillian, probably all seven. Rufinus, Augustine, and Jerome, the last with some reservations, acknowledged the full canon of seven. Jerome is careful to observe that II and III John are ascribed not to John the apostle but to John the presbyter of Ephesus. But as with Hebrews, his inclusion of them in his Vulgate version outweighed these halting reservations.

It was indeed that version which virtually determined the canon of the west. It was Jerome who separated the books of the Greek Old Testament which were extant in Hebrew from those known to him only in Greek, distinguishing the latter as the Apocrypha and thus giving them a place of limited authority in the canon of scripture. In the Greek Bible they had been on an equality with the rest but to this the learning of Jerome had seen that they were hardly entitled. His revised New Testament of twenty-seven books undertaken at the instance of Pope Damasus, and thus having behind it the prestige of the Roman church, completed the victory of Hebrews and the longer list of Catholic letters in the west.

The decrees relating to the New Testament books supposed to have been issued by various early popes, Damasus (366–84), Gelasius (492–96), and Hormisdas (514–23), have proved to be really no earlier than the sixth century. The one claiming the name of Pope Gelasius contains our present New Testament books, but with the Catholic letters following the Revelation.[8] Its maker thought it necessary to forbid the reading of a long series of apocryphal works —gospels, acts, and apocalypses—which he lists to the number of forty.

Yet about the middle of the sixth century (560), Cassiodorus, who had been prime minister of Theodoric and in his old age founded a monastery at his home in Southern Italy for the preservation of the old learning, copied from an "old translation" a list of New Testament books which omitted Hebrews and included only three of the Catholic letters—Peter, James, and John.[9] This made a New Testament of twenty-two books, like the earliest Roman list and that of the Syriac Peshitto, although not identical with either of these in the precise twenty-two books included. Cassiodorus was a native of Southern Italy, but his family was of Syrian origin and this may account for his interest in the short list of Catholic letters, so like that of the Peshitto version. His "old translation" shows how persistent and widespread was the conservative attachment to the shorter New Testament.

In the centuries that followed the Greek New Testament was seldom copied in a single volume. Manuscripts of the four gospels were common, but manuscripts containing the gospels, Acts, epistles, and Revelation were very rare. The connection of the Revelation with the Greek New Testament was therefore a very loose one. Indeed, our Greek manuscripts of the Revelation are decidedly few in number. Greek manuscripts containing the gospels are seven times as numerous as those containing the Revelation, and in about half of these latter the Revelation stands alone unaccompanied by any other New Testament books. The New Testament was, in fact, usually a set of books rather than a single volume, and the set was seldom complete. Leontius of Byzantium, in his lectures delivered at a convent in Jerusalem about 530, says that the New Testament consists of six books, or volumes: (1) Matthew and Mark; (2) Luke and John; (3) Acts; (4) the seven Catholic letters; (5) the fourteen letters of Paul; and (6) the Revelation of John. To Leontius and to most Greek Christians of the Middle Ages, the New Testament was not so much a book as a shelf of books.

In the west, on the other hand, manuscripts of the whole New Testament in the Latin Vulgate version were very numerous. The twenty-seven books were usually copied into one volume, and this physical fact both expressed and intensified the western conception of them as a unit. Thus the thousands of Latin manuscript New Testaments that exist show more conclusively than the official list of any council could do the triumph in the west of the Athanasian canon of the New Testament.

XV

THE MIDDLE AGES

STEP by step the New Testament had risen to a position of equality with the Jewish Bible and even of superiority to it. For the New Testament was not interpreted to harmonize with the Old but the Old to agree with the New.

Upon the books that belonged to the New Testament the main divisions of the Christian church were formally at least in agreement. The most influential opinion of the Greek and Latin churches had, after long fluctuation, come practically to rest upon the canon of twenty-seven books fixed by Athanasius in his festal letter of 367 and included by Jerome in his revision of the Latin Bible. The Syriac and Ethiopic New Testaments differed strikingly from both these and still more from each other. The Syriac Peshitto continued to be copied through the Middle Ages with only twenty-two books in its New Testament, omitting the Revelation and the four minor Catholic letters. The Ethiopic New Testament, on the other hand, contained thirty-five books, the twenty-seven of our list being followed by eight others—the so-called Clement and the Synodus. As we have seen, Clement included among other things an expanded form of the ancient Revelation of Peter. It is from it indeed that the fullest text of that mysterious work has very recently been obtained.

This strange appendix to the New Testament is early reflected (about 400) in a Greek list of the New Testament books which included eight books of the so-called Apostolical Constitutions—summaries of church law issued in Clement's name which it was ecclesiastically convenient to have appended to the list of New Testament books. But this combination is not heard of after the sixth century, and through the Middle Ages the Greek New Testament remains practically unchanged. Its principal use was to be read in the churches, and those books like the Revelation from which no church lessons were taken were little read. Yet Andreas of Caesarea in Cappadocia probably in the sixth century produced a commentary on the Revelation, evidently regarding it as a New Testament book. His was the first commentary on the Revelation produced in the east, if we except some recently discovered scholia upon it by Origen.

To the sixth century belongs also the curious figure of Cosmas called Indicopleustes because his voyages took him to the borders of India. At first a traveling merchant, he became in later life a monk of Sinai and a writer on theology and geography, greatly concerned to prove that the earth was not round but flat. His journeys had given him large opportunities of observation, and he records that among the Syrians only three Catholic letters are accepted—James, Peter, and John. Cosmas himself regarded all the Catholic letters with suspicion and tried to show that they had never had an established place in the New Testament. Some of Cosmas' archaeological observations have proved to be correct, but his views on the canon seem to have had little influence.

One of the most interesting documents in the history of the New Testament is the list of books of the Bible that bears the name of Nicephorus, patriarch of Constantinople (†828).[1] It is usually known as the Stichometry of Nicephorus, because it gives the length of each book in *stichoi* or lines of Homeric length, in which Greek manuscript books were usually measured. In its present form the list probably comes from Jerusalem and about the middle of the ninth century. Nicephorus somewhat like Eusebius classes the books as canonical or disputed, and the Revelation is in his disputed list.

One of the most striking figures in the Greek Renaissance of the ninth century was Photius, first captain of the guard and later patriarch of Constantinople. The final rupture of the Greek and Latin churches centered about him, but he is not less notable for his contributions to learning. He wrote a series of estimates, or, as we should call them, reviews, of two hundred and eighty works of Greek literature, including many quotations sometimes of considerable length. A great many of the works he discusses have been lost and so we owe to this so-called Library of Photius practically all that we know about many classical and early Christian writers. Photius accepted the Revelation as a part of New Testament scripture.

Arethas, a later successor of Andreas at Caesarea (about 900), and like Photius a figure in the Greek revival of the time, also commented upon the Revelation as scripture. Arethas based his commentary upon that of Andreas, and in many of the extant Greek manuscripts of the Revelation his commentary accompanies it.

We have seen the New Testament take on a

certain fixity of form in the east, largely in con-
sequence of the weight of Athanasius' influence.
In the west it was the great name of Augustine
that most contributed to its complete acceptance, happily combined with Jerome's great revision, the Vulgate. The figure of Augustine
brooded majestically over the Latin Christianity of the Middle Ages. Jerome's Vulgate,
however, came slowly into general use, and not
until the ninth century was its supremacy over
older forms of the Latin text established. It is
hard to realize that the greatest of all the versions took five hundred years to achieve complete success.

The most curious variation in the canon of
the west in the Middle Ages relates to the Letter
to the Laodiceans. At the close of the Letter to
the Colossians Paul speaks of a "letter from
Laodicea," of which nothing is known. As early
as the fourth century someone undertook to
compose from familiar Pauline phrases, mostly
from Philippians, a short letter about the length
of III John, to meet this description.[2] It was
probably written in Greek, and its name appears
in a Greek manuscript of the ninth century just
after Philemon, but without its text, which we
know only in translations. In Latin it is found

in perhaps a hundred manuscripts, first of the earlier Latin New Testament and then of the Vulgate, from the sixth century down. Jerome speaks of it with disdain, as rejected by all. The Spanish Priscillian (†385) thought it was a genuine work of Paul, but was not scripture. Filastrius of Brescia toward the close of the fourth century thought it was a genuine work of Paul, but should not be read in church. Pope Gregory the Great (about 600) thought it genuine but not entitled to a place in the New Testament. In Britain, Alfric, abbot of Cerne (989), accepted it as a fifteenth letter of Paul, and John of Salisbury (1165) believed it to be Paul's. It was even translated into Old English and German, and stood just after Galatians in all the High German Bibles from 1466 until Luther. It was also translated into Arabic. As late as 1600 it was discussed in lectures at Tübingen, and the distinguished French scholar Faber Stapulensis (Lefèvre d'Etaples) (†1536) included it among the letters of Paul.

Another slight local disturbance in the western canon occurred in Spain where the Visigoths had brought their version of the New Testament made by Ulfilas about the middle of the fourth century and without the Revelation. The influence of this shorter Gothic New Testament in Spain called forth the denunciation of the fourth Council of Toledo in 633, which excommunicated any who did not accept the Revelation as scripture.

A number of Latin New Testament manuscripts include the Latin version of the Shepherd of Hermas. But these were only ripples in the smooth course of the Latin New Testament. The bull of Pope Eugene IV in 1441 reaffirming the canon of Augustine laid down more than a thousand years before shows how really fixed the canon of the west remained through the Middle Ages.

The Middle Ages saw the Latin Bible pass more and more into the hands of the clergy and become more and more fixed. Bishops and councils frowned upon the idea of translating it into the languages spoken in Western Europe. It remained the peculiar possession of the educated, who of course knew Latin. The Synod of Toulouse in 1229 forbade the laity to have books of the Old or New Testament, except perhaps the Psalms, and prohibited the translation of the Bible into the vulgar tongue. In 1233 the Synod of Tarragona declared that no one should possess books of the Old or New Testament in

Romance. The emperor Charles IV in 1369 recognized that the laws of the church forbade lay people of either sex to read any books whatever of Holy Scripture written in the vulgar tongue. When Tyndale's translation of the New Testament reached England in 1526 the Archbishop of York reminded Henry VIII that "All our forfadres of the church of England hath with all diligence forbid and eschued publication of English bibles." In all this the Roman Catholic position that the church is the sole interpreter of scripture is evident.

So it came about that the New Testament had by no means the importance in the Middle Ages that it had possessed before. It was now subordinated to the church and greatly restricted in influence. Its contents were accepted as long since settled. Men did not inquire on what grounds a given book had been included in the New Testament. The problems about it which had so concerned early Christian scholars did not exist for those of the Middle Ages. Thomas Aquinas and Nicholas of Lyra read of some of them, it is true, in Jerome or other Fathers, but such questions did not interest the medieval mind. They had a vague impression that they had all been settled by the time of the

Council of Nicaea in 325. The Bible was still considered inspired, but only in a very accommodated sense, as part of the tradition of the church. Authority lay now with the church rather than with the scripture.

The very languages in which the Bible was written were forgotten. Greek became a dead language. In the west no one understood it or could read it. The Greek New Testament was looked down upon as inferior to the authorized Latin Vulgate, and when Cardinal Ximenez in 1514–17 published the Greek and Hebrew Old Testaments in parallel columns in his Complutensian Polyglot he set the Latin Vulgate text between them, as he remarked in his Preface, like Jesus between the two thieves. To such positions had ignorance and dogmatism brought the Latin church.

XVI

THE AGE OF PRINTING

THE invention of printing gave to the New Testament and to the whole Bible a new and more definite unity. The first book to be printed was the Latin Bible. Printing at once tended to fix the form of the New Testament in both text and contents, and thus put the finishing touch to the long process of canonization.

But the same great movement of the awakening human mind, which found one expression in the art of printing, had other consequences not less important for the New Testament. Interest in it revived. New translations were wanted and produced. Most Catholic authorities frowned upon such translations, but courageous and far-seeing men like John Wyclif even before the invention of printing had begun to translate the Bible from Latin into modern tongues, and no less than eighteen German Bibles, based on the Latin Vulgate, appeared between 1466 and 1522.

Notable encouragement was given to these modern-language versions by the great Erasmus, who in 1516 expressed the hope that the Greek

New Testament would be translated into all spoken languages and be read by men and women.[1] This wish was soon followed by Luther's German New Testament of 1522 and Tyndale's English one of 1525. Erasmus himself published a new Latin translation of the New Testament, which was almost as amazing a thing to do as translating it into English would have been.

Even more important was the new interest in Greek which led Cardinal Ximenez in Spain (1514) and Erasmus in Switzerland (1516) to print the Greek text of the New Testament. Greek began to become known to Italian literary men like Boccaccio toward the close of the fourteenth century, but it was not taught in the University of Paris until after the middle of the fifteenth century (1458) and made its appearance at Oxford thirty years later (1491). The Fall of Constantinople before the Turks in 1453 drove many learned Greeks to take refuge in Italy and the west. Many Greek manuscripts found their way into the hands of western scholars and were published in print. All this belongs to the story of the Renaissance, but its relation to the history of the New Testament is very close.

The new interest in Greek sources of culture

naturally involved a new interest in the early literature of Christianity and a return from the medieval indifference to the New Testament, to the old emphasis upon it.

All these interests combine in the figure of Erasmus. He spoke for the modern-language versions when it was not the fashion to do so. He learned Greek and was the first to publish the Greek text of the New Testament. He was bold enough to make a new Latin translation from the Greek, as though the old Latin Vulgate were not good enough; and he raised questions about the canon of the New Testament which had not been seriously faced for a thousand years.

Nicholas of Lyra (†1340) has been called the greatest biblical interpreter of the Middle Ages. He stands almost on the threshold of the Renaissance, and we find him raising problems about the New Testament which had long slumbered undisturbed. Nicholas discusses the question whether Paul wrote Hebrews and marshals arguments on this side and on that. It is true he settles the question mainly by appealing to the authority of the church, but it was something that he raised it at all.

The men of the sixteenth century, however, were no longer disposed to accept the New Testament simply as a part of tradition, but again began to inquire on what grounds its several books had been admitted to it. The old questions which had been left unsettled and forgotten for so many centuries as to the authorship of Hebrews, James, II Peter, II and III John, Jude, and Revelation, caught the attention of Erasmus. The doubts about Hebrews, which had been expressed by the greatest men of the Middle Ages—Thomas Aquinas (†1274) and Nicholas of Lyra (†1340)—had impressed Erasmus more than the easy way in which they had satisfied them. His own studies led him to conclude that Paul could not have written Hebrews, nor Peter II Peter, and that it was John the Elder, not the apostle, that wrote II and III John. Erasmus was also very doubtful about Jude, since it quotes an apocryphal book, and he could not think the Revelation the work of John the Evangelist.

In all this, Erasmus was guided by literary considerations, on the one hand, and by the observations of early Christian writers, on the other. He did not rush to the conclusion that books which he could not accept as apostolic must forthwith be excluded from the New Testament. But he exercised the right to test the apostolic claims of each book for himself, and in so doing he resumed the task left unfinished by Jerome and his generation, and struck the old dogmatic conception of the New Testament as a collection of apostolic scripture a staggering blow.

Churchmen with humanist leanings like Cardinal Cajetan were also awakening to the old problems. Cajetan, who as the Pope's legate examined Luther at Augsburg, went far beyond Erasmus in his criticism. Like Laurentius Valla (†1457), from whose writings Erasmus learned so much, he recognized that the Vulgate was only a human translation, and while he clung to the doctrine of verbal inspiration he gave up the allegorical interpretation that had so long gone with it. The old doubts expressed by Jerome and echoed by Erasmus as to Hebrews and II and III John, Cajetan felt and acted upon. If the Pauline authorship of Hebrews was uncertain, then its canonicity and its authority were uncertain. II and III John and Jude were likewise of less authority than the "certain" scriptures. In this procedure, Cajetan felt that he was faithfully following Catholic tradition, as embodied in one of its greatest figures, Jerome.

But the great awakener of new thought about

the New Testament was Luther. For him the final authority lay not with councils nor popes but only with the word of God. He declared the Bible the single and complete source of doctrine. Even in the Middle Ages voices had not been altogether wanting that declared the scripture the Christian's sole authority, but they had been voices crying in the wilderness, like the Waldenses. Luther brings this idea forward with a new keenness and vigor. For him the New Testament was authoritative because it taught Christ and brought salvation and peace to the soul.

Luther accordingly judged the books of the New Testament by this new standard: Did they teach Christ? If they did they were "apostolic," no matter who wrote them. This was very much like what the ancient church had done; it had found ways of making out as apostolic whatever books had seemed valuable enough to deserve to be apostolic. That is, its judgments had been practical rather than historical. Luther approached each book of the New Testament from the point of view of its practical religious value. With him it was not literary considerations or tradition but religious values that mattered.

Thus approached, the New Testament books

in Luther's mind fell into various groups. The best ones were the Gospel of John, some letters of Paul—especially Romans, Galatians, and Ephesians—I Peter, and I John. These Luther considered the heart of the New Testament. On a slightly lower level he placed the gospels of Matthew, Mark, and Luke, the Acts, II Peter, II and III John, and the other letters of Paul. These were the principal books of the New Testament, and they all taught Christ.

Apart from these stood a third class which Luther judged much less favorably, as not teaching Christ—Hebrews, James, Jude, and the Revelation. Among these he found more worth in Hebrews and Jude than in James and the Revelation. In the Revelation he found too little about Christ, and too much that no one could understand. Luther compared it to IV Ezra which he once said he threw into the Elbe. In comparison with the other books of the New Testament, he considered James "an epistle of straw." He did not indeed omit these four books which he so disapproved from his New Testament, but he put them at the end of it in the order Hebrews, James, Jude, Revelation, and in his Table of Contents he did not number them with the other books, but set them off apart from the rest without numbers. This makes it plain that he did not regard them as entitled to stand on an equality with the others, the "principal books" of the New Testament. And they still stand in the modern German Bible at the end of the New Testament, where Luther placed them.

Luther's unfavorable view of these four books found echoes in the work of William Tyndale, who in his English translation of the New Testament (1525) follows Luther in putting Hebrews and James just before Jude and Revelation, and not numbering these four with the rest.[2] The early printings of the English Bible—Coverdale (1535), Thomas Matthew (1537), and Taverner (1539)—follow Tyndale in adopting Luther's order. But in later printings, beginning with the Great Bible of 1539, the older order reappears. Yet the Geneva Bible of 1560 says of Hebrews that it is not likely that Paul wrote it. The Thirty-nine Articles of 1562–71 assume the New Testament canon as fixed for the Church of England, and the three Authorized Bibles of 1539, 1568, and 1611, culminating in the long reign of the King James Version, established it in fact as well as in theory.

John Calvin of Geneva (†1564) knew the difficulties attaching to these doubtful books of the New Testament as well as anyone, but they did not greatly interest him. The minor books in question seemed to him to contain nothing unworthy of a disciple of Christ, and this fact combined with their traditional position in the canon satisfied him of their canonicity. He may have felt differently as to the Revelation; at any rate, he wrote no commentary upon it. Theodore Beza, Calvin's successor at Geneva, held similar views, taking the objections to these books even less seriously than Calvin had done.

Over against these humanists and reformers, the Roman Catholic Council of Trent in 1546 dealt with the questions of tradition and scripture which the Reformation had so acutely raised. The twenty-seven New Testament books contained in Jerome's Latin Vulgate were declared scripture, and of equal authority. The letters of Peter, John, James, and Jude and the Revelation of John were definitely declared apostolic; the Latin Vulgate was fixed as the authoritative form of the New Testament, and the tradition of the church declared of equal authority with scripture.

Thus in the conflict about the contents of the New Testament which was one of the results of the humanist movement, the Catholic church clung to the position of the Middle Ages, which had known only the Vulgate and virtually if not consciously esteemed tradition and scripture alike. The invention of printing had fixed the scope of the New Testament with a definiteness and uniformity impossible before; and the human mind, freed by the Renaissance and the Reformation, had resumed those investigations into New Testament origins on which it is still engaged.

XVII

THE NEW TESTAMENT APOCRYPHA

WHEN Jerome made his revision of the Latin Bible, toward the end of the fourth century, he put the books of the Greek Old Testament which were not in the Hebrew Bible in a group by themselves and called them the Apocrypha. The New Testament has no such appendix; there are, strictly speaking, no New Testament Apocrypha. But there are books not in our New Testament which at various times and in some localities have been considered part of it, and their temporary connection with it throws some light upon the way in which it was regarded. They formed a kind of fringe or border about the New Testament, the study of which is very instructive.[1]

The earliest forms of the New Testament as they emerged in Rome and Alexandria toward the close of the second century included not only a collection of gospels and a collection of Pauline letters, but a collection of revelations as well. The Roman church and the churches under its immediate influence at first accepted not only the Revelation of John but the Revelation of Peter or the Shepherd of Hermas or both. These ancient apocalypses did not long hold a place in the New Testament, but their influence can be traced not only in the third and fourth centuries but a thousand years later in the works of Dante himself.

The Shepherd was one of the most popular books produced in the early church. It was a collection of the visions of Hermas, a Christian prophet of Rome, in most of which a rugged figure dressed like a shepherd was his guide. From this the book took its name, the Shepherd. The visions were written at intervals through the life of Hermas, and toward 150 they were gathered together to form the Shepherd as we have it. Like the Revelation of John, it was expressly intended to be read in church. Its claim to be the work of a prophet made it natural for Roman Christians to consider it scripture, but it is a revelation of quite another type than that of John or Peter. It is really an earnest plea for repentance which the prophet addressed to the Roman church.

In Alexandria the Shepherd was at first highly esteemed. Clement prized it and regarded it as well as the revelations of John and

of Peter as scripture. Origen, too, accepted it.
The Shepherd stands in the Clermont list of the
books of the New Testament which represents
Egyptian usage about 300, but it is one of the
four books—Barnabas, the Shepherd, the Acts
of Paul, the Revelation of Peter—marked with
a dash as doubtful. I Peter is also marked with
a dash, but probably for another reason. Eusebius, about 325, puts the Shepherd among the
disputed books which are rejected. Its popularity in the east is already on the decline. Athanasius recommends it for private reading by
catechumens and new converts, but excludes it
from the New Testament. Yet it stands at the
end of the New Testament in the great Sinaitic
Bible Manuscript which comes from his times.

The western churches knew the Shepherd
well. Irenaeus of Lyons considered it scripture.
The Muratorian writer, about 200, says it may
be read, but not in church among the prophets
or apostles, because it was written recently by
Hermas (who was not an apostle), and as the roll
of the prophets is closed it cannot be included
among them. Tertullian of Carthage, our third
early western figure, after he became a Montanist condemned the Shepherd in unmeasured
terms for what he considered its moral laxity.

The Shepherd was never afterward officially accepted as scripture in the west. Jerome said that it was almost unknown among the Latins. In the sixth-century Roman list which goes under the name of Pope Gelasius, the Shepherd is one of the forty books condemned as apocryphal. But it was early translated into Latin and continued to be copied all through the Middle Ages, often actually as part of the Latin Bible.

The Revelation of Peter was written in Greek early in the second century. It shows the influence of Greek ideas of rewards and punishments in a future life. The little book seemed to have disappeared completely, when in 1886 a manuscript containing more than a third of it was found in a grave at Akhmim in Upper Egypt. With the aid of that discovery, the whole text has since been found imbedded in the books which under the name of Clement stand after the Revelation of John in the Ethiopic New Testament.

The Muratorian writer accepted it as scripture. Clement of Alexandria commented upon it in his Outlines as part of the New Testament. Hippolytus knew it at Rome in the third century but not as a part of the New Testament. In the east it was more than once quoted as scripture in the fourth century, but Eusebius placed it among the books that were disputed and rejected. Sozomen, who wrote his Church History about 450, says that in his day it was still read once a year in the churches of Palestine, on Good Friday, although it was "considered utterly spurious by the ancients." The Clermont list, of the sixth century, marked it with the stroke with which it designated books of doubtful canonicity, and some have thought this marking may have stood in the original list, made in Egypt about 300, of which the Clermont list is a copy. In the list of Nicephorus, coming from Jerusalem about 850, the Revelation of Peter stands among the "disputed books of the New Testament"—the Revelation of John, the Revelation of Peter, the Letter of Barnabas, and the Gospel according to the Hebrews.

The failure of the Revelation of Peter to hold its place in the Roman and Alexandrian New Testaments will surprise no one who reads it. Its repulsive and detailed descriptions of the punishments of hell fell too manifestly short of the standards of religious literature set by the four gospels and the letters of Paul. Moreover, it was of no such antiquity as most of the books that made up the first New Testament, and these drawbacks even its claim of the great name of Peter could not overcome.

The Revelation of Peter was one of a whole cycle of books bearing the name of Peter, most of which at one time or another had a place in the New Testament. There was a Gospel of Peter, Acts of Peter, two letters of Peter, the Preaching of Peter, and the Revelation of Peter. There was actually enough of this literature to compose a New Testament of Peter, but of course these books were never assembled into such a group.

The Preaching of Peter was the earliest Christian apology, or defense of Christian life and doctrine against pagan attack. It was written very early in the second century, and was considerably imitated in the Apology of Aristides a generation later. The complete work has disappeared, so that it is best known to us through a few fragments preserved in Clement of Alexandria. Clement regarded it as a genuine work of Peter and quotes it just as he does I Peter, so that it may fairly be said to belong to his New Testament. His Gnostic contemporary, Heracleon, also quoted it, but Origen and Eusebius saw that it was not from Peter's hand and rejected it. But the strange saying of Jesus to the apostles which it contained, "After twelve years go forth [from Jerusalem] into the world," was the basis of much later opinion as to the early movements of the Twelve.

The Teaching of the Apostles is another book quoted as scripture by Clement. It originated about the beginning of the second century as a series of moral injunctions—"You must not commit adultery, ... You must not practise magic, ... You must not desire anything of your neighbor's," and the like—to be taught to Christian converts from paganism. This was expanded by the middle of the century by the addition of a little manual of church life—how to baptize, fast, observe the Eucharist, and conduct public worship. This primitive little work had a widespread influence in the early church, and it is not strange to find it quoted as scripture by Clement of Alexandria. But Origen does not include it in his New Testament, and Eusebius puts it among the books that are disputed and rejected. Athanasius omits it from the New Testament but says that it, like the Shepherd of Hermas, may be read by catechumens and new converts. In the so-called List of Sixty Canonical Books and also in the Stichometry of Nicephorus it is listed among the "apocrypha";

but in both these lists the "apocrypha" are the rejected books, and do not include what we ordinarily call the Apocrypha of the Old Testament.

The Letter of Barnabas is another book which had a place in the New Testament of Clement of Alexandria. It was written about 130, and is chiefly remarkable for its extreme allegorical treatment of the Old Testament. The writer says the Jewish Law was never intended to be taken literally but only figuratively. Origen followed Clement in accepting Barnabas as scripture, and in the Sinaitic Manuscript, of the fourth century, Barnabas stands immediately after the Revelation of John. The Clermont list has it at the end of the Catholic letters, between Jude and the Revelation of John, but marks it with a dash. Eusebius classes it as disputed and rejected; Athanasius omits it altogether. The List of the Sixty Canonical Books mentions Barnabas among the rejected books, the apocrypha, but the Stichometry of Nicephorus (850) places it among the disputed books, with the Revelation of John, the Revelation of Peter, and the Gospel according to the Hebrews; not among the rejected ones, such as the Gospel of Thomas, the Teaching of the Apostles, and Hermas. In the west it seems never to have had any canonical position. Jerome speaks of it with respect; he believes it is the work of Barnabas, but it is not a part of the New Testament. He classes it among the "apocryphal writings," but this is not, with Jerome, a term of condemnation.

Another book which Clement accepted as scripture is the Letter of Clement of Rome to the Corinthians. This was written by the Roman church toward the end of the first century to the church at Corinth, where Roman Christians felt the presbyters were not sufficiently respected. It was probably part of the response of the Roman church to the stirring challenge of Hebrews that it take up the task of teaching the churches. This I Clement sets out to do, without much genius but at great length.

Clement's successors in Alexandria did not accept I Clement as scripture. Origen, Eusebius, and Athanasius had no place for it in their New Testaments, although they knew it well enough. Eusebius believed it was written by Clement, the third bishop of Rome, but does not really count it even among the disputed books of the New Testament.

Even before the time of Clement, this letter was read in church at Corinth, as Dionysius, bishop of Corinth, says in writing to Soter, bishop of Rome, about 170. Dionysius is answering a letter from Soter, and it is perhaps Soter's letter to him that became anciently attached to I Clement and came to pass for a second letter of Clement, though it is plainly a little homily or sermon. At any rate, the two so-called letters passed under the name of Clement into the Alexandrian Manuscript of the Greek Bible, of the fifth century, where they follow the Revelation of John. They are mentioned as part of the New Testament in the Apostolic Canons, a Syrian work of about 400. They stand also in a twelfth-century Syriac Manuscript of the New Testament, in which they follow the Catholic letters and precede those of Paul. And Abu'l Barakat (†1363) in his account of Christian Arabic literature speaks of the two letters of Clement as belonging to the New Testament. But the Stichometry of Nicephorus (850) classes them not among the disputed books but with the rejected ones, its "apocrypha."

The Acts of Paul also for a long time had a precarious place on the fringes of the New Testament. It was written by a Christian presbyter of Asia about 170 and gave a somewhat romantic account of Paul's missionary wanderings and escapes. Its most famous chapter was that about Paul and Thecla, but the further correspondence of Paul with the Corinthians which stood in Efrem's New Testament was also a part of it.

Origen and Hippolytus both knew the Acts of Paul, but not as part of the New Testament. Tertullian rejects it with vehemence. It begins Eusebius' list of rejected writings. In the Clermont list it stands between the Shepherd and the Revelation of Peter, and is marked like them with a dash. In the Stichometry of Nicephorus five hundred years later, it again begins the list of rejected books (apocrypha) under the title of the "Journey of Paul."

The various versions had their peculiar additions to the New Testament. The part played by the Letter to the Laodiceans in some Latin New Testament manuscripts and early German Bibles has already been described. The Syriac in Efrem's day, the middle of the fourth century, had III Corinthians. The Ethiopic had the eight books of Clement and the Synodus, in which along with various ecclesiastical regulations, the Revelation of Peter was imbedded. This very much resembles the effort made in Syria about 400, in the Apostolic Canons, to add to the New Testament the two letters of Clement and the eight books of church law known as the Apostolical Constitutions. John of Damascus (†about 750) placed the Apostolic Canons and perhaps the two letters of Clement at the end of the New Testament.

It is plain that no ancient New Testament included all these doubtful books. The list of books of the Bible given in the Clermont Manuscript, probably representing the practice of Egypt about 300, after listing the four gospels, the letters of Paul, and seven Catholic letters, gives Barnabas (marked with a dash), the Revelation of John, the Acts of the Apostles, the Shepherd, the Acts of Paul, and the Revelation of Peter—the last three marked like Barnabas with a dash as doubtful books. The similar dash before I Peter in that list probably means only that the Catholic letters begin with it.[2] Eusebius a little later lists as rejected from the New Testament the Acts of Paul, the Shepherd, the Revelation of Peter, the Letter of Barnabas, the Teachings of the Apostles, and as he dubiously remarks, "the Revelation of John, if it seem proper," although he himself regards this as an accepted book. This was early in the fourth century. The Sinaitic Manuscript of the Greek

Bible, written perhaps half a century later, has Barnabas and the Shepherd after the Revelation of John. About the same time (367) Athanasius recommends the Teaching of the Apostles and the Shepherd as a kind of appendix to the New Testament, on a par with the Old Testament Apocrypha and suitable for new converts to read. The Alexandrian Manuscript of the Greek Bible, written in the fifth century, has the two letters of Clement after the Revelation of John.

Three famous lists remain. The Roman one bearing the name of Gelasius but probably belonging to the sixth century follows the New Testament with a list of some forty rejected and heretical works, including the Gospel of Peter, the Shepherd, and the Acts of Paul and Thecla, which are to be avoided by Catholics.[3] The perplexing List of the Sixty Canonical Books mentions twenty-six New Testament books, leaving out the Revelation of John.[4] In this it resembles Gregory of Nazianzus and the sixtieth canon of Laodicea in the fourth century —both voices from Asia Minor. As "outside or beside the Sixty," it gives nine books that we class as Old Testament Apocrypha but none for the New Testament. As "apocrypha" in its own sense, that is, as rejected, it names fourteen Jewish books and eleven Christian, including the Revelation of Peter, the Letter of Barnabas, and the Acts of Paul. The absence of the Revelation of John from the list is strange especially as the Revelation of Peter and even the later Revelation of Paul are mentioned.

The Stichometry of Nicephorus, reflecting the practice of Jerusalem about 850, after giving the Four Gospels, the Acts, fourteen letters of Paul, and seven Catholic letters, lists as the disputed books of the New Testament the Revelation of John, the Revelation of Peter, the Letter of Barnabas, and the Gospel according to the Hebrews.[5] Its rejected list, or "apocrypha" in its own sense, includes the Journey of Paul, the Teaching of the Apostles, the two letters of Clement, and Hermas.

Such was the debatable ground over which the tide of the New Testament ebbed and flowed in the early centuries, and so uncertain was the line that in Christian antiquity separated this literary borderland from the accepted books of the New Testament.

XVIII

THE NEW TESTAMENT TODAY

WE HAVE seen the primitive collections of Christian books and letters that were most valued in the early church gathered up toward the close of the second century into a New Testament, to stand as a companion to the Old Testament and to serve the needs of private devotion, public worship, and ecclesiastical controversy. Supposedly apostolic in origin, they could be appealed to in debate with the schismatics as authentic records of Christian beginnings. They were read in church along with the Old Testament, but in actual use the New Testament now dominated the Old, which was interpreted to agree with it.

In canonizing the New Testament the ancient churches in a sense did no more than recognize a condition that already existed. Many of its books had long been familiar and were in general use in public worship and private devotions. To proclaim these a New Testament was hardly more than to acknowledge their existing status. From another point of view, however, canonization was a decided change. It placed the books of the New Testament upon a footing of authority, as the writings of inspired apostles, of which the most of their writers had never dreamed, and upon a footing of equality which tacitly assumed that they were in entire harmony with one another on all points, and in effect suppressed the possibility of difference. Where there was difference, the view that agreed with tradition prevailed, and the rival opinion was ignored. This inevitably led to dangerous mental habits.

Canonization naturally cut off the New Testament books from their historical origins and treated them as independent of human conditions of composition and superior to them. It was enough that they were apostolic writings. It made them something that they had not been before and saw in them peculiar values which neither their writers nor their earlier readers had recognized. For the idea of great personalities possessed and guided by the spirit of God it substituted the idea of books inspired by that spirit. It was now the literature instead of the history that had been inspired.

The canonization of from twenty-two to twenty-seven books as the New Testament led to the neglect of other early Christian books, then to their condemnation, and finally to their disappearance. Much of undoubted value in early Christian literature was thus allowed to perish. On the other hand, it insured the preservation of documents of extraordinary primitiveness and value like the letters of Paul, which otherwise might have been lost.

And while the conception of the collection as of equal authority in all its parts tended to a mechanical harmonization of the various books with one another and to the blurring of their characteristic contours, and so dulled the understanding of them, the books themselves carried with them in much of their teaching a mental vigor and spiritual vision that perpetually checked the effort to conventionalize them. The stirring call to freedom in Galatians and the idea of the perpetually enlarging grasp of truth in John made themselves felt from generation to generation, in spite of theological dogmatism and religious conventionality.

The dogmatic idea that all parts of the New Testament are necessarily of equal authority does not stand the practical religious test, as Luther long ago saw. No amount of ecclesiastical dogma can make Jude equal to I Peter or the Sermon on the Mount. The idea of equal authority failed to reckon with the differences of opinion and point of view within the New Testament and set the devout reader the impossible task of agreeing with men who did not always agree with one another. Modern historical study of these books in the light of the situations in which they were written helps us to understand these differences and brings us closer to the religious experience of which the books are an expression.

This dogmatic conception of the New Testament was seriously re-examined by the humanists and reformers. Literary questions were reopened and books estimated afresh in terms of sheer religious worth. More and more the modern world has been interested in the science of introduction; who wrote a given book, why he wrote it, in what circumstances, with what materials, and for whom. This approach is in part occasioned by the belief that the worth of the book to us depends upon our understanding of it, and our understanding of it depends on our knowledge of just such matters as these. It is not so much the mere words of those ancient figures that will help us as the understanding of their religious tasks and problems and the spirit in which they approached them. Never were the books of the New Testament more diligently studied than in modern times. The modern student and reader wishes to go behind the old dogmatic verdict to the origins of the books and learn the mind of each author. In such an understanding of the New Testament he believes he will find values more real and great than those of the older dogmatism.

The modern world is not disposed to alter the New Testament. It has been wrought into the warp and woof of modern literature, modern thought, and modern life too deeply for that. For centuries the best minds of the Christian world have been focused on its pages with a concentration that would have made even a lesser literature classical. We shall not give up the New Testament nor any part of it. It is part of the fabric of the modern world.

But that rigorous re-examination to which the modern world has subjected all its inheritances has not overlooked the New Testament, and if the New Testament has come out of that scrutiny without loss of prestige it is not because of what has so long been claimed for it dogmatically, as the inspired work of apostles, but because of its incomparable moral challenge and its unequaled religious appeal. The old indiscriminate regard for the letter of the New Testament has given way to a deeper and more vital reverence for the life, ideals, and hopes of which it is the expression.

In the New Testament some things were said better than they had ever been said before or have ever been said since. In setting these things conspicuously before the eyes of the Christian world the canonization of the New Testament did an immeasurable service. It was in fact fundamentally in recognition of these values that the New Testament books were thus exalted. Experience had shown that most of them possessed extraordinary religious worth. This was the religious basis of canonization, and to it modern religious feeling eagerly responds. To the ecclesiastical and dogmatic interest which combined with this in the formation of the New Testament, in the not unnatural effort to conventionalize Christianity, modern thought is indifferent. But its chief interest is for the life which these books reflect and for the message which that life has for our own.

We have in a sense been repeating the process of the second century, and evaluating these earliest books of Christian literature afresh for ourselves. This is why our minds turn back to the story of the formation of the New Testament and ask how and why the collection was first made. The attitude of Clement of Alexandria who saw inspiration wherever he found truth strikes a responsive chord in us. We have seen what a variety of New Testaments existed in the fourth and fifth centuries—how Athanasius had one, and Chrysostom another, and Theodore a third. And in a sense every man today has his own New Testament, made up of the books which above all others give him the religious inspiration he needs.

It is undeniable that the modern mind is undoing the work of canonization in the dogmatic sense. It would go back to that life of the spirit with which Christianity began. Christianity began as a religion of spirit, and the resort to a canonized scripture like the Old Testament was really a decline from the bolder, freer, higher life of faith with which it had begun. It is part of the earnestness and courage of modern Christianity that it is ready to relinquish the artificial exaltation of the New Testament to return to the simple faith and love which were its first ideals.

But if we must deny to the New Testament the old dogmatic claims made for it by its first framers, it is only to give a deeper understanding to its great individual voices which they muffled into an unreal agreement or muzzled altogether. The great formative period of Christianity speaks to us with a clearness and nearness impossible to the old dogmatism. The writers of the New Testament speak to us today more plainly and convincingly than they have spoken since the second century. It has been finely said that the New Testament has again and again brought dogmatics back to history, and never has it been truer than in our day. The historical approach to the books of the New Testament has deepened our sense of the human sympathy and understanding between the New Testament times and our own, and correspondingly enriched modern religious life.

For the old mechanical treatment of the New Testament it has given us an organic vital appreciation. These books are not vast masses of independent mottoes but each is a powerful coherent argument or narrative, richly freighted with religious experience and inspiration. We no longer resort to the New Testament merely to look up references or support our doctrines. We go to it to share the life and problems and achievements of the early church, and in the great presence of Jesus to feel again his inspiration and power. It is not the religious authorities set up by the second century but the religious inspiration and help of Christianity's creative period that we feel the need of today, and that we find in the New Testament.[1]

NOTES

CHAPTER I

¹ The origin of the several books of the New Testament can be conveniently surveyed in my *Story of the New Testament*, or in Fowler, *The History and Literature of the New Testament*.

² See List 3.

³ See I Cor. 2:15, 16; 3:16.

⁴ See Clement of Alexandria, *Stromateis* ("Scrap-books") vi. 4.

⁵ Compare also the Egyptian Book of the Dead, the books of Musaeus and Orpheus, and especially the religious use of Homer in those times.

⁶ *Against Apion* i. 8.

⁷ See Swete, *Introduction to the Old Testament in Greek*.

⁸ II Tim. 3:16.

CHAPTER II

¹ I Cor. 7:25, 26; II Cor. 11:17.

² The use of Mark by Matthew and Luke can be seen in Burton and Goodspeed, *Harmony of the Synoptic Gospels*.

³ Compare Luke 1:1-4.

⁴ The day of the Crucifixion (in relation to the Passover), the time of the cleansing of the Temple, and the number of Jesus' visits to Jerusalem are out standing examples.

⁵ Rev. 1:3.

⁶ Rev. 22:18.

⁷ Eph. 2:20; 3:5.

⁸ See Lake, *The Apostolic Fathers*.

⁹ See James, *The Apocryphal New Testament* ,p. 505.

¹⁰ I Cor. 12:28.

¹¹ Heb. 5:11—6:1.

NOTES

[12] Compare Jude with II Peter, chap. 2.

[13] II Pet. 3:15, 16.

[14] II Pet. 1:14-18.

CHAPTER III

[1] Rev. 1:4—3:22.

[2] See Lake, *The Apostolic Fathers*, Vol. I.

[3] See the Letter of Polycarp to the Philippians, chap. xiii, in Lake, *The Apostolic Fathers*, Vol. I.

[4] See Page, *Thirteen Epistles of Plato*.

[5] Philostratus *Life of Apollonius* i. 7; iv. 27; v. 39-41; vii. 35, etc.

[6] I Clem. 47:1; Ignatius, Eph. 12:2; Polycarp, Phil. 3:2.

[7] They are Romans, I Corinthians, Ephesians, Philippians, Galatians.

[8] For he has in chap. 5 a very different list of Paul's hardships from that in II Cor. 11:23-33.

[9] See List 1.

[10] See Lists 2 and 3.

[11] The Vatican and Sinaitic manuscripts of the fourth century.

[12] Ignatius, Eph. 12:2.

[13] Romans, chap. 16.

[14] Note the harsh change at Phil. 3:2 and the different situations reflected in chaps. 2 and 4.

[15] For as a collection they are subsequent to Acts but prior to Revelation.

CHAPTER IV

[1] Note the phrase "remember the words of the Lord Jesus" in Acts 20:35; I Clem. 13:1.

[2] Acts 20:35.

[3] Polycarp, Phil. 7:2.

[4] For it is first clearly reflected in Ignatius of Antioch.

[5] Though several other orders, especially Matthew, John, Luke, Mark, appear here and there in manuscripts and lists.

[6] See especially Teaching 11:3, 4, and compare Matt. 10:40, 41, to which it refers.

[7] John 21:25.

[8] The discovery of a Latin version of this original form of the Teaching shows that it was not Jewish but Christian, and was called not the Two Ways but even then the Teaching of the Apostles.

[9] See Lake, *Apostolic Fathers*, Vol. II.

[10] Cf. Matt. 5:1, 2; Bar. 2:6: "The new law of our Lord Jesus Christ."

CHAPTER V

[1] See article, "Marcion," by Harnack, in *Encyclopaedia Britannica*.

[2] *Apology* xxvi. 5.

[3] *Against Marcion*, Book v.

[4] See List 2.

[5] Many Latin manuscripts of Paul's letters contain Marcionite prologues to the several letters; see Souter, *Text and Canon*, pp. 205–8.

CHAPTER VI

[1] *Apology* lxvii. 3.

[2] *Dialogue* xxix. 2.

[3] *Apology* lxvi. 3.

[4] *Dialogue* ciii. 8.

[5] *Dialogue* cvi. 3.

[6] II Pet. 1:15.

[7] *Dialogue* lxxxi. 4.

[8] II Pet. 3:16.

[9] See chap. xiii.

[10] Eusebius *Church History* iv. 29. 6.

NOTES

CHAPTER VII

[1] *On the Resurrection* 18.
[2] *Plea for the Christians* ix. 1.
[3] *To Autolycus* i. 14.
[4] iii. 12.
[5] ii. 9.
[6] ii. 22.

CHAPTER VIII

[1] *Against Heresies* (or, as Irenaeus called it, the *Refutation of Gnosticism*) iii. 3. 2, 3.
[2] *On Prescription against Heretics* 36.
[3] See List 3.
[4] In the Latin Codex Fuldensis, about 546 A.D.
[5] *On Modesty* 10.
[6] Eusebius *Church History* v. 16. 3.

CHAPTER IX

[1] Oxyrhynchus Papyri, I, 1.
[2] *Church History* vi. 14. 1.
[3] *Address to the Greeks*, ch. 8.
[4] Eusebius *Church History* vi. 14. 2–4.
[5] See List 19.
[6] See List 7.
[7] *Scrap-Books* vi. 15.
[8] *Scrap-Books* i. 20.
[9] *Scrap-Books* iii. 13.

CHAPTER X

[1] Eusebius *Church History* vi. 23. 2.
[2] Eusebius *Church History* vi. 25. 1.
[3] So Jerome, translating Origen's remark on Luke 1:1.
[4] Eusebius *Church History* vi. 25. 8, 12.
[5] See List 7.
[6] Hippolytus (Achelis ed.), p. 231, l. 10.

FORMATION OF THE NEW TESTAMENT

CHAPTER XI

[1] *Church History* vii. Introduction.
[2] *Church History* vii. 25.
[3] *Church History* vi. 32. 3.
[4] *Church History* iii. 25.
[5] See List 5.
[6] See List 4.

CHAPTER XII

[1] See List 8.
[2] See List 7.
[3] See List 19.

CHAPTER XIII

[1] *Church History* iv. 29. 6.
[2] *Church History* vi. 12.
[3] See Burkitt, *Evangelion da Mepharreshe.*
[4] See List 15.
[5] See List 16.
[6] See List 17.

CHAPTER XIV

[1] See List 10.
[2] See List 11.
[3] See List 12.
[4] See List 13.
[5] See List 6.
[6] See List 9.
[7] See List 14.
[8] See List 20.
[9] See List 21.

CHAPTER XV

[1] See List 23.
[2] See Westcott, *History of the Canon*, Appendix E, for its Latin text.

NOTES

CHAPTER XVI

[1] In the Preface to his Greek Testament.
[2] See List 24.

CHAPTER XVII

[1] See Lake, *Apostolic Fathers*, and M. R. James, *The Apocryphal New Testament.*
[2] See List 4.
[3] See List 20.
[4] See List 22.
[5] See List 23.

CHAPTER XVIII

[1] See Scott, *The New Testament Today*; Fosdick, *The Modern Use of the Bible*; and Harnack, *The Origin of the New Testament*, Part II.

BIBLIOGRAPHY

WESTCOTT, B. F. *A General Survey of the History of the Canon of the New Testament.* London: Macmillan, Seventh ed., 1896. (A standard descriptive treatment of the subject, with valuable lists.)

MOORE, E. C. *The New Testament in the Christian Church.* New York: Macmillan, 1904. (Eight lectures on the rise and place of the New Testament.)

GREGORY, C. R. *The Canon and Text of the New Testament.* New York: Scribner's, 1907. (A descriptive treatment, conversational in style.)

SOUTER, A. *The Canon and Text of the New Testament.* New York: Scribner's, 1913. (A concise treatment with valuable Appendix of documents.)

HARNACK, A. *The Origin of the New Testament.* New York: Scribner's, 1925. (A stimulating presentation of some of the main problems of the canon.)

LEIPOLDT, J. *Geschichte des Neutestamentlichen Kanons.* 2 vols. Leipzig: Hinrichs, 1908. (The best systematic modern German treatment of the canon.)

JACQUIER, E. *Le Nouveau Testament dans l'Eglise Chrétienne: I. Préparation, Formation et Définition du Canon du Nouveau Testament.* Paris: Lecoffre, 1911. (The best modern French work on the canon.)

MILLIGAN, G. *The New Testament Documents, Their Origin and Early History.* London: Macmillan, 1913.

MOEHLMAN, C. H. *The Unknown Bible.* New York: Doran, 1926.

SCOTT, E. F. *The New Testament Today.* New York: Macmillan, 1921.

FOSDICK, H. E. *The Modern Use of the Bible.* New York: Macmillan, 1924.

HISTORIC LISTS

1. The Letter Collections of John and of Ignatius
2. The Canon of Marcion
3. The Muratorian Canon
4. The Clermont List
5. The List of Eusebius
6. The Cheltenham List
7. The List of the Sinaitic Manuscript
8. The List of Athanasius
9. The List of Jerome
10. The List of the Synod of Carthage
11. The List of Chrysostom
12. The List of Gregory of Nazianzus
13. The List of Amphilochius of Iconium
14. The List of Augustine
15. The List of the Teaching of Addai
16. The Sinaitic Syriac List
17. The List of the Peshitto Syriac Version
18. The List of the Ethiopic Version
19. The List of the Alexandrian Manuscript
20. The List of the "Decree of Gelasius"
21. The List of the "Old Translation" known to Cassiodorus
22. The List of the Sixty Canonical Books
23. The List of the Stichometry of Nicephorus
24. The List in Tyndale's New Testament

187

FORMATION OF THE NEW TESTAMENT

1. THE LETTER COLLECTIONS OF JOHN AND OF IGNATIUS

John to the Seven Churches of Asia

 Ephesus
 Smyrna
 Pergamum
 Thyatira
 Sardis
 Philadelphia
 Laodicea[1]

Ignatius to

 Ephesians
 Magnesians
 Trallians
 Romans
 Philadelphians
 Smyrnaeans
 Polycarp[2]

2. THE CANON OF MARCION (ABOUT 140 A.D.)

Luke
Galatians
Corinthians (I, II)
Romans
Thessalonians (I, II)

Laodiceans (=Ephesians)
Colossians
Philippians
Philemon

3. THE MURATORIAN CANON

(Discovered and published by L. A. Muratori in 1740 from a Milan manuscript of about 800. It represents the usage of Rome about 200 A.D. The lines dealing with the first and second gospels are missing, but Luke is numbered the third.)

[1] Rev. 1:4, 11 (90-95 A.D.).   [2] 107-17 A.D.

188

HISTORIC LISTS

[Matthew]
[Mark]
Luke
John
Acts of All the Apostles
Corinthians (I, II)
Ephesians
Philippians
Colossians
Galatians
Thessalonians (I, II)
Romans
Philemon
Titus
Timothy (I, II)
(Laodiceans and Alexandrians are spurious)
Jude
John (I, II)
Wisdom of Solomon
Revelation of John
Revelation of Peter (which some reject)
(The Shepherd of Hermas may be read but not publicly in
   church)

4. THE CLERMONT LIST

(From the sixth-century Graeco-Latin Codex Claro-
montanus, representing probably the usage of Egypt about
300. The list in Latin stands after the Letter to Philemon.)
(We omit the Old Testament list, Genesis-Tobit)
   Four gospels:
   Matthew
   John

Mark
Luke
Letters of Paul:
Romans
Corinthians (I)
Corinthians (II)
Galatians
Ephesians (Philippians, Thessalonians [I, II], and per-
    haps Hebrews also, probably omitted here by mistake
    of the scribe)
Timothy (I)
Timothy (II)
Titus
Colossians
Philemon
—Peter (I)
Peter (II)
James
John (I)
John (II)
John (III)
Jude
—Letter of Barnabas
Revelation of John
Acts of the Apostles
—Shepherd
—Acts of Paul
—Revelation of Peter

(The dash before I Peter may be only a "paragraph-
us," or Greek paragraph mark, to suggest that I Peter
and the items that follow are not part of the "Letters of
Paul.")

HISTORIC LISTS

5. THE LIST OF EUSEBIUS

(From his *Church History* iii. 25 [about 325 A.D.]).

The "accepted" books:

  Four gospels

  Acts of the Apostles

  Letters of Paul

  John (I)

  Peter (I)

  Revelation of John ("if it seem proper")

The "disputed" books:

  James

  Jude

  Peter (II)

  John (II, III)

The "rejected" books

  Acts of Paul

  Shepherd

  Revelation of Peter

  Letter of Barnabas

  Teachings of the Apostles

  Revelation of John ("if it seem proper"; see above)

  Gospel according to the Hebrews

6. THE CHELTENHAM LIST

(Discovered by Mommsen in 1885 in a manuscript then at Cheltenham, England. Believed to represent the usage of North Africa about 360 A.D. Omitting the estimates of length the New Testament part runs:

Four gospels:

Matthew	John
Mark	Luke

FORMATION OF THE NEW TESTAMENT

Letters of Paul XIII	Letters of John, three
Acts of the Apostles	one only
Revelation	Letters of Peter, two
	one only

7. THE LIST OF THE SINAITIC MANUSCRIPT OF THE GREEK BIBLE (ℵ)

(Written about the middle of the fourth century.)

Gospel:

	Hebrews
According to Matthew	Timothy (I, II)
According to Mark	Titus
According to Luke	Philemon
According to John	Acts
Romans	James
Corinthians (I, II)	Peter (I, II)
Galatians	John (I, II, III)
Ephesians	Jude
Philippians	Revelation of John
Colossians	Letter of Barnabas
Thessalonians (I, II)	Shepherd

8. THE LIST OF ATHANASIUS

(Festal Letter 39) (367 A.D.)

Four gospels:

According to Matthew
According to Mark
According to Luke
According to John
The Acts of the Apostles
Catholic Letters of the Apostles VII:
James

Peter (I, II)
John (I, II, III)
Jude
Letters of Paul the Apostle XIV:
Romans
Corinthians (I, II)
Galatians
Ephesians
Philippians
Colossians
Thessalonians (I, II)
Hebrews
Timothy (I, II)
Titus
Philemon
The Revelation of John

(Apart from these and not in the list, the Teaching of the Apostles, and the Shepherd [grouped with the Wisdom of Solomon, the Wisdom of Sirach (= Ecclesiasticus), Esther, Judith, and Tobit].)

9. THE LIST OF JEROME

(Letter 53) (about 394 A.D.)

Matthew
Mark
Luke
John
Paul "wrote to seven churches (for an eighth to the Hebrews is put outside the number by very many); he instructs Timothy and Titus and appeals to Philemon on behalf of a runaway slave."
Acts of the Apostles

Seven letters of James, Peter, John, and Jude
Revelation of John

10. THE LIST OF THE SYNOD OF CARTHAGE (397 A.D.)

Four gospels	John, three
Acts	James
Letters of Paul XIII	Jude
The same to the Hebrews	Revelation of John
Peter, two	

11. THE LIST OF CHRYSOSTOM

(Synopsis of Holy Scripture) (Chrysostom died in 407 A.D.)

Fourteen letters of Paul
Four gospels, John and Matthew, Luke and Mark
The Book of Acts
Three Catholic letters

12. THE LIST OF GREGORY OF NAZIANZUS

(On the Genuine Books of Inspired Scripture [Gregory died about 390 A.D.]. After putting down what he describes as twenty-two books of the Hebrew scriptures, Gregory mentions:)

Matthew, Mark, Luke, John
The Acts of the Apostles
Fourteen Letters of Paul
Seven Catholic letters:

   James
   Peter, two
   John, three
   Jude
"You have them all."

13. THE LIST OF AMPHILOCHIUS OF ICONIUM

(Lines to Seleucus [Amphilochius died after 394 A.D.].)

Matthew
Mark
Luke
John
Acts of the Apostles
Fourteen letters of Paul:
  Romans
  Corinthians, two
  Galatians
  Ephesians
  Philippians
  Colossians
  Thessalonians, two
  Timothy, two
  Titus
  Philemon
  Hebrews (which some mistakenly reject)
Of Catholic letters some say seven, and others only three,
    James, Peter, and John; the former add II Peter,
    II and III John, and Jude.
The Revelation of John some accept but the majority
    reject.

14. THE LIST OF AUGUSTINE

(On Christian Doctrine ii. 13 [Augustine died 430 A.D.].)
Four gospels:
  According to Matthew
  According to Mark

According to Luke
According to John
Fourteen Letters of Paul:
  Romans
  Corinthians (I, II)
  Galatians
  Ephesians
  Philippians
  Thessalonians (I, II)
  Colossians
  Timothy (I, II)
  Titus
  Philemon
  Hebrews
Peter (I, II)
John (I, II, III)
Jude
James
Acts of the Apostles
Revelation of John

15. THE LIST OF THE TEACHING OF ADDAI (ABOUT 350 A.D.)

The New Testament of the Diatessaron
The Letters of Paul
The Acts of the Twelve Apostles

16. THE SINAITIC SYRIAC LIST (ABOUT 400)

Matthew, Mark, Luke, John
Acts
Fourteen letters of Paul
"This is all."

HISTORIC LISTS

17. THE LIST OF THE PESHITTO SYRIAC VERSION (ABOUT 425 A.D.)

Matthew, Mark, Luke, John
Acts
Fourteen letters of Paul
Three Catholic letters: James, Peter, John

18. THE LIST OF THE ETHIOPIC VERSION

The four gospels
Fourteen letters of Paul
Seven Catholic letters
Acts
Revelation of John
Clement and the Synodus (eight books)

(The order in manuscripts is sometimes Paul—Acts—Revelation—Catholics, and sometimes Catholics—Revelation—Acts—Paul.)

19. THE LIST OF THE ALEXANDRIAN MANU-SCRIPT OF THE GREEK BIBLE (A)

(Fifth century; this Table of Contents somewhat later.)
Gospels:
  According to Matthew
  According to Mark
  According to Luke
  According to John
Acts of the Apostles
Catholic letters: Seven
Letters of Paul: Fourteen
Revelation of John
Clement, Letter I

Clement, Letter II

"Altogether, ... Books." (The number is lost in a hole in the parchment.)

Psalms of Solomon: Eighteen

(The last are now wanting in the manuscript, but mentioned in the Table of Contents as an Appendix.)

20. THE LIST OF THE "DECREE OF GELASIUS" (SIXTH CENTURY)

Four gospels:

    According to Matthew

    According to Mark

    According to Luke

    According to John

Acts of the Apostles

Fourteen letters of Paul:

    Romans

    Corinthians, two

    Ephesians

    Thessalonians, two

    Galatians

    Philippians

    Colossians

    Timothy, two

    Titus

    Philemon

    Hebrews

Revelation of John

Seven "canonical" letters:

    Peter, two

James
John, three
Jude

(Some forms of the list separate I John as the work of John the Apostle from II and III John which are ascribed to John the Presbyter, or Elder.)

21. THE LIST OF THE "OLD TRANSLATION" KNOWN TO CASSIODORUS

(From his *Institutio Divinarum Litterarum*, chap. xiv, about 560 A.D., where he describes this list as that of an "old translation")

Four evangelists: Matthew, Mark, Luke, John
Acts of the Apostles
Letters:
  Of Peter to the Nations
  Of James to the Twelve Tribes
  Of John to the Parthians
Letters of Paul:
  Romans
  Corinthians, two
  Galatians
  Philippians
  Colossians
  Ephesians (Some texts add Hebrews here)
  Thessalonians, two
  Timothy, two
  Titus
  Philemon
Revelation of John

FORMATION OF THE NEW TESTAMENT

22. THE LIST OF THE SIXTY CANON-ICAL BOOKS

(The New Testament books are Nos. 35–60.)

The Gospel:
  According to Matthew
  According to Mark
  According to Luke
  According to John
Acts of the Apostles
Letter of:
  James
  Peter
  Peter
  John
  John
  John
  Jude
Paul to:
  Romans
  Corinthians
  Corinthians
  Galatians
  Ephesians
  Philippians
  Colossians
  Thessalonians
  Thessalonians
  Timothy
  Timothy

Titus
Philemon
Hebrews
 Apocrypha
  (After 14 Old Testament apocrypha)
History of James
Revelation of Peter
Travels and Teachings of the Apostles
Letter of Barnabas
Acts of Paul
Revelation of Paul
Teaching of Clement
Teaching of Ignatius
Teaching of Polycarp
Gospel according to Barnabas
Gospel according to Matthias

23. THE LIST OF THE STICHOMETRY OF NICEPHORUS (ABOUT 850 A.D.)

Gospel according to Matthew
Gospel according to Mark
Gospel according to Luke
Gospel according to John
Acts of the Apostles
Fourteen letters of Paul
Seven Catholic letters:
 James
 Peter, two
 John, three
 Jude

"Disputed" books:
  Revelation of John
  Revelation of Peter
  Letter of Barnabas
  Gospel according to the Hebrews
"Rejected" books (Apocrypha):
  Journey of Paul
  Journey of Peter
  Journey of John
  Journey of Thomas
  Gospel according to Thomas
  Teaching of the Apostles
  Clement I and II
  Ignatius, Polycarp, and Hermas

24. THE LIST OF TYNDALE'S NEW TESTAMENT (1525)

(Evidently influenced by Luther's New Testament of 1522.)

The bokes conteyned in the
newe Testament.

i The gospell of saynct Mathew
ii The gospell of S. Marke
iii The gospell of S. Luke
iiii The gospel of S. Jhon
v The actes of the apostles written by S. Luke
vi The epistle of S. Paul to the Romans
vii The fyrst pistle of S. Paul to the Corrinthians
viii The second pistle of S. Paul to the Cortinthians
ix The pistle of S. Paul to the Galathians.
x The pistle of S. Paul to the Ephesians.

xi The pistle of S. Paul to the Philippians
xii The pistle of S. Paul to the Collossians
xiii The fyrst pistle of S. Paul unto the Tessalonians
xiiii The seconde pistle of S. Paul unto the Tessalonians
xv The fyrst pistle of S. Paul to Timothe.
xvi The seconde pistle of S. Paul to Timothe.
xvii The pistle of S. Paul to Titus
xviii Te pistle of S. Paul unto Philemon
xix The fyrst pistle of S. Peter
xx The seconde pistle of S. Peter
xxi The fyrst pistle of S. Jhon
xxii The seconde pistle of S. Jhon
xxiii The thryd pistle of S. Jhon
> The pistle unto the Ebrues
> The pistle of S. James
> The pistle of Jude
> The revelacion of Jhon.

INDEX

FORMATION OF THE NEW TESTAMENT

INDEX

INDEX